MW01256803

THOUGHTLESS MAGIC AND MANIFESTATIONS

THOUGHTLESS MAGIC AND MANIFESTATIONS

Through Non Verbal Protocols

RICHARD DOTTS

© Richard Dotts 2015
1ˢᵗ edition
ISBN-13: 9781519125439
ISBN-10: 1519125437
Questions / comments? The author can be contacted at
RichardDotts@gmail.com

TABLE OF CONTENTS

CHAPTER ONE

LET THE UNIVERSE BLESS YOU!

I am so excited to be writing this next book and to be sharing all that I have learned so far with you. This book which you are now holding in your hands, represents an exploration of uncharted territory that is right at the cutting-edge of human consciousness. Why do I say so? During the past decade of seriously studying the works of the great spiritual masters, I haven't found more than a handful of books which have touched on these subjects, and even then, only briefly.

This book continues in the direction set by two of my earlier books, "Light Touch Manifestations" and "Infinite Manifestations." If you have read those two books, you are in good stead, as we deepen our discussion of these Universal principles and spiritual laws in the pages to come. If you are a new reader of my work, my hope is that you'll find something of value here as well. My intention is to have every reader learn a practical "spiritual" skill which they can immediately apply to improve their own lives. I have written this book so that little background knowledge is necessary. All that is needed is an open mind—and oftentimes, a beginner's mind (free from any and all expectations) works best.

I am heartened to find that readers have found my previous books on the subject of manifestations useful. What is even more heartening is that we have progressed together through these books, deepening our understanding of the creative process and these manifestation principles. While we may have only met through these pages, I take great delight in reading the emails and correspondences which you have sent me. Although my personal schedule does not allow me to reply to each and every one of you, each of you is in my prayers and blessings. As I have written before, we are all in this together—so let's help each other as much as possible!

Many of you have written about your success stories and unique personal experiences. Those are great learning experiences for me as I fine-tune my own understanding and communication of these spiritual laws. Some of you have written asking me for help in various areas of your life, but I would like to remind you that the greatest power lies within yourself. Deep within you are creative abilities so powerful that once accessed, will allow you to break through any challenge or problem you face in your life. In fact, once you have successfully "broken through" and created a new reality for yourself, you will wonder why you had not applied these methods sooner, since you have always been blessed with these abilities.

I can group readers of my books into three broad categories. The first group of readers are those who have—in their own ways and through their own focus—"graduated" from this material. By applying the techniques and principles in their own lives, they have managed to create more desired realities for themselves and have broken away from their past conditioning. Readers in this first group will find problems spontaneously disappearing from their lives. What remains is a pure, joyful journey with pleasing manifestations at every turn. Almost everything in their life pleases them now. More often than not, these readers find little need to continue reading these (or similar) books. They have finally found the everlasting peace and success which they had so yearned for previously, and have now achieved for good. Quite a number of readers from this group stay on to learn how to fine-tune their own vibrations, but by-and-large, the major kinks in their lives have all been sorted out.

Readers from the second group are those who are completely new to this material. They may have read similar self-help literature in the past and may have grown weary of trying all the techniques, only to find things returning to square one after a while. Understandably, these readers are the most skeptical and cynical of the lot. They also have a lot of pent-up frustration and resistance within themselves, which makes it more difficult for them to achieve their desired results. I was once in this group. While my desire to achieve outer success was very great, I had also built up a lot of negative expectations, disappointments and false beliefs about the world along the way. All of these worked against me as I was trying to improve my life for the better.

The good news for the second group of readers, is that this book goes directly to the heart of the matter. We will discuss highly effective ways to deal with inner resistance, which is preventing you from getting what you want. This inner resistance may show up in the form of faulty beliefs, negative emotions or feelings, and unwanted thoughts. Once you learn how to completely eliminate these self-defeating inner thoughts from your inner state and life, the positive results which you seek will come very quickly.

The third group of readers are those who are currently in-between. They were once like the second group of readers; disappointed and weary from their journey, but things are changing for the better. Their world is showing signs of improvement and change. Things are starting to get better. For this third group, the concepts which you learn in this book will greatly accelerate that change, but only if you are faithful in applying the methods. It is important not to get caught up in old programming and old beliefs as you apply this material towards building your new life.

My life really started to change after I read a few hundred success and self-help books. Ironically, my life did not change because of what was written in those books, but because of what was *not* written in those books. Each book I read would advocate a new set of techniques or a new method to try, for which I would follow religiously for the following two weeks or so. Thereafter, seeing no results from those techniques, I would discard them in favor of finding the next secret or magic potion that would help me. Sound familiar?

Many people who write to me today still ask about that one 'magic' technique or step to help them get what they want. They must be thinking that I am withholding some stuff from my readers! But as I have written many times before, there are no hidden secrets. The secrets are out there in plain view for everyone to see and use, yet few ever take the time to practice and apply it faithfully to their own lives. Why? They have somehow convinced themselves that the "secret" must be something much more obscure and complicated, such that it can only be known by a privileged few. Therefore, the simple and profound truth laid out in front of them can never be the glamorous "secret" which they are looking for.

As I wrote in my book "Your Greatest Gift," it was only after reading hundreds of self-help books and out of sheer exhaustion that I reached the opposite conclusion. By then, I had read almost all of the classics as well as the acclaimed modern works. I reasoned that if the secret was to be found within them, I would have found it—for I had read everything, and I had tried to get my hands on every piece of external knowledge ever known to mankind. And yet, the secrets to creating a successful life were not found in any of those.

I reasoned then that the secret had to be something *within* us, something so fundamental that every single human being on this planet could access at a moment's notice. When I came to this realization, I felt goosebumps all over my body; it was as if my higher self was intuitively confirming this truth, which I had arrived at by logic. I later found confirmation of this in the works of the great spiritual and religious masters, who have repeatedly taught that our greatest potential lies latent within ourselves; waiting to be discovered.

How do we activate these latent creative abilities that lie within ourselves, waiting to create abundant lives? By arriving at the earlier realization, I have already ruled out the reliance on external knowledge or external sources of information. This is a point that I will return to later in our discussion, but for now, what I mean is that we do not need any external knowledge or technology (that is not already a part of ourselves) to manifest whatever we want in life.

This is important, so I'll repeat it again: There is nothing external that you need in order to create whatever you want in your life. As a born creator, everything that you need for this purpose is already *within yourself.* You already possess the body and mind which you need for the creative experience, and there is no external knowledge or information which you need to seek out. What you do need to learn (actually *un*learn) is how to use this apparatus which you have been blessed with.

I discovered that each time I had an intention and held it purely in my consciousness, that intention came true extremely quickly in my outer reality, with almost no time delay. Therefore, I could think about something I wanted, and depending on whether I thought about it and felt the associated feelings purely enough in my body…whatever I intended would appear in my life just as quickly.

This discovery was a true epiphany to me. It was also what caused me to write this series of books to share what I have learned with others. To someone who has received a Western scientific education all his life, being able to influence matter with the use of my own mind was something shocking and completely out of my belief system. What's more, my training taught me to only believe in objective phenomena that could be accurately measured and quantified. Such inner phenomena and inner states are beyond the current realms of science. This is why I have chosen to call this a form of "magic"—for the results you can achieve are nothing short of magical!

The intention behind my previous books was to show readers how to cultivate an inner state of peace that is conducive to our outer manifestations. You would have noticed that I place a lot of emphasis on the word "pure" in my descriptions above, for it is only with the purest of intentions that we can manifest whatever we want and create our desired conditions in the outer world.

What do I mean by pure? A state of purity refers to the absence of negative beliefs, negative feelings and contradictory thoughts in our consciousness that prevent us from thinking about what we want in a focused way. Negative thoughts and feelings scatter our focus, leading to little or no results when trying to create our desired good.

For example, if you want to experience greater financial abundance in your life but are constantly swarmed with worrying thoughts about your finances, you are not holding on to your primary intention for abundance purely enough. This is what prevents the successful fulfillment of your desires. The solution then is to get rid of those negative feelings and limiting beliefs that frequently bother you as you go about your life, as those prevent the speedy manifestation of your desires.

Those who have achieved results from my other books will know that manifestations are not about taking particular actions or using particular techniques. There is nothing you have to do specially in order to get what you want, so there is no need to keep using affirmations, visualizations or vision boards if these activities do not make you feel good about what you are asking for. All of these physical actions per se do not lead to the fulfillment of your desires. Neither will the words and incantations which you utter in your prayers make things happen any faster. The only things which influence your outer manifestations are your inner state and the feelings which you feel on the inside during the majority of your day.

Therefore, if using certain techniques makes you feel particularly joyful as you focus on your desires, then by all means continue using them. But for most people, these artificial means only serve to magnify their existing feelings of worry and desperation on the inside. They are using these techniques not from a place of pure joy and inner peace, but from a place of impatience and desperation, that of wanting things to happen faster for them. As one's outer reality always matches up to their dominant inner states, this can only result in more circumstances to feel worried or desperate about.

What is needed are effective ways of eliminating all our worrisome thoughts, negative beliefs and counter-intentions. Once these have been dealt with, then the physical fulfillment of our desires happen very easily. The whole creative process becomes as simple as holding an intention for something in our consciousness and then watching it happen on the outside with little or no involvement on our part. This is true no matter what you ask for.

This process of eliminating negative feelings, thoughts and beliefs from our inner states differs slightly from one person to the next. Some people will have an easier time giving up their negative, unwanted feelings than others. For example, upon learning that negative feelings impede our outer manifestations, some individuals will be able to let go of their self-defeating thought patterns and beliefs just like that. These are the individuals for whom results often show up the quickest, as they are able to exercise effective control over their own inner states. They simply make a conscious decision to not *think* like the past, and make it happen.

For the rest of us, change may not happen so easily. It can be difficult to work against the negative conditioning and thought patterns that have become ingrained in us over several decades of our lives. We may find it difficult to break out of our life-long habits of incessant worrying, complaining, criticizing, blaming and feeling resentful about ourselves or others. We may find it difficult to remove our feelings of doubt and just trust in the process. This is why some of us may still find negative thoughts and feelings lingering in our consciousness despite the tremendous amount of inner work that we have done. This is natural, since we are working against decades of negative conditioning, much of which was picked up when we were still young and unable to discern truth from falsehood. Add to that any traumatic incidents which we may have gone through, which often lead to the formation of unresourceful, self-sabotaging beliefs that distort our perception of life.

And now, for the most exciting part of our journey together: In the past decade of my life and since the time I developed a greater appreciation for the nature of our creative reality, I have sought to communicate the fastest and most effective ways through which we can break through these negative mental patterns that hold us back. The more work I do in this area, the more I realize that there is a way out of everything, which I have described above.

No matter what your personal circumstances may be at the moment, no matter how your physical reality may seem to you right now…everything can change in an instant. If you could find a way to drop all your negative thoughts, feelings, emotions and limiting beliefs this very instant…if you could find a way to clear out your mental cache and reset yourself to *zero*, then the desired life which you have always yearned for will come into being very quickly.

And that is what we are discussing in this book. New, cutting-edge, and never-before-published techniques for dropping all of our inner resistances that prevent our outer manifestations from happening. In our time together, you will learn powerful new methods for getting rid of unwanted and unresourceful beliefs just like that—with the snap of a finger. You will learn how to bypass all the unnecessary logical rationalizations, bad feelings and negative beliefs that have plagued you for years on the inside. You will learn how to deal with the mind chatter and silence it effectively. You will, in essence, learn skills which have only come from years of deep and disciplined meditation.

All of this is not new. The greatest spiritual masters have alluded to various forms of this practice throughout the ages. What is new here are the effective and practical ways through which we can integrate this timeless information into our modern lifestyles. Living in this new way requires a certain willingness to give up some of your preconceptions about the world, which I believe you possess, since you have already picked up this book.

If you read this book while keeping yourself open to all possibilities, then you'll find that all things will happen in ways that pleasantly surprise you! Let's get started.

Chapter Two

Towards a Unified Framework for Manifestations

In order for us to understand each other, it is necessary to first outline a basic framework for manifestations through which our discussions will be based upon. This framework will be familiar to existing readers of my books, and it is mainly included here so that new readers can get up to speed.

We have already established in the previous chapter that we live in an intentional Universe. This means that the Universe picks up on the feelings and intentions which we hold on the inside and it responds accordingly. In fact, "picking up" is not the appropriate phrase to use here, since we are literally at one *with* the Universe. We are the Universe and the Universe is us. We are the sum total of the entire Universe. Therefore, there is nothing for the Universe to "pick up" on, just as it would be somewhat absurd to say that "John is picking up on his own thoughts." There is nothing for John to pick up, since John and "himself" are the same entity and John always knows what his thoughts are in each moment.

I have explained this in previous books as having an always-on connection to the Universe. When
you have an always-on connection to the Internet (as
is the case with many high speed Internet connections nowadays), there is no need to dial-up to the
Internet and disconnect when you are done. You'll
find that the Internet connection is right there for
your usage when you fire up your browser. It may
even be downloading your emails in the background
as you work on your documents. Our relationship
with the Universe works in very much the same way.
Since we are one *with* the Universe, we are literally
inseparable from it. Every inner thought, intention
or feeling we experience on the inside is shaping
Universal energy and causing some kind of energetic response. The initial effects of this energetic
response often come in the form of feelings we
experience on the inside. For example, if we hold an
angry thought in mind, we automatically *feel* angry.
This *feeling* of anger is an energetic response to the
angry thoughts which we hold on the inside.

Most people dismiss these energetic responses as
mere feelings. This is why we pay very little attention
to them and generally disregard them. Some people
have no qualms with feeling angry, bitter, resentful,
self-critical or worried all day, because they perceive
these as mere feelings which they hold on the inside
which will never amount to anything tangible. **This is
the biggest mistake one can possibly make**. The feelings which you experience on the inside are not just
mere feelings. They are pure and powerful energetic

vibrations which subsequently **go on to affect your outer states and outer reality**. Therefore, if you allow yourself to be steeped in angry thoughts all day, you are sending out clear and coherent intentions for anger. This results in more outer circumstances, events and people to feel angry about, leading to a downward negative spiral that can be very difficult to get out of.

Contemporary self-help literature has called this phenomenon the Law of Attraction. While the Law of Attraction (LOA) has entered mainstream self-help culture, it has been very much misinterpreted, leading to much confusion. For now, it is sufficient to recognize the relationship between LOA and the manifestation framework which I have just described above.

One of the issues with the modern LOA frame-work is its focus on the "attraction" part of the equation, as its name suggests. The use of the word "attraction" seems to suggest that there are things we need to actively do in order to attract the good into our lives. This is why a whole industry has been built up around the techniques, actions and methods which one can take to attract their desires in a shorter time. These range from the use of visualizations, affirmations, meditations, self-hypnosis or tapping, to more esoteric and unorthodox techniques. There is often a comparison of which techniques work better and are more effective, with readers scrambling to find the latest technique that has a higher success rate. Something that is also happening is the twisting of existing self-help material to fit into the LOA perspective.

All of this has led to much confusion for readers. As I have explained in my books, manifesting your desires is *not* about the use of outer actions, techniques, methods or mantras. Manifestations are not about what you do on the outside. They are not about physical actions you take to "attract" your good. In fact, there is nothing to "attract" in the first place when you are already one *with* the Universe!

Manifestations are your birthright. This means that everyone is born with the ability to create the life of their dreams and to have absolutely joyous and fulfilling experiences in their lifetime. We do not need to behave in certain ways in order to "attract" the good into our lives. All of our good is already here for our taking. Unfortunately, many people unknowingly impede their own progress by spending an inordinate amount of time on daily visualizations and affirmations, trying to coerce some higher power into giving them what they believe is withheld from them. This is just not how the Universe works. Nothing you ask for is ever withheld from you.

Since manifestations are our birthright, the ability to create something always lies within us. This ability is something so fundamental to our being that it can never be taken away from us. We may have forgotten *how* to tap into this ability along the way, but it can be rediscovered very quickly. All we need to do is to hold a pure intention on the inside with sufficient focus and then allow what we have asked for to come into our lives in the most harmonious ways. Accepting this Universal truth is probably the first hurdle for most people, since we have been taught to believe that good things only come through hard work and struggle. As such, we are closed off to avenues which do not require physical actions.

A quick look at your own life will expose the fallacies behind such thinking. Have there been things in your life which you have not achieved despite lots of well-meaning hard work and struggle? Perhaps you have not achieved the level of financial abundance or career success that you hoped for, despite putting in many hours and trying to do everything right. This is the first indication that merely working harder is not the answer to what we are looking for.

On the other hand, have there been good things which happened serendipitously in your life with little or no active intervention on your part? Again, you will find this to be the case. A friend once told me that some of the best and most fortuitous things in his life happened almost by chance, with no intervention on his part. He could not have possibly foreseen them or made them happen by working harder. Things just happened. These are not mere coincidences, but signs of a greater Universal intelligence at work, nudging us towards our greater good. As I write in my book "Manifestation Pathways," there are no accidents in this Universe. Wouldn't it be wonderful if we could all live like that, from one spontaneous miracle to the next?

No amount of foresight would have allowed me to foretell my own unique career paths, although I consider myself to be quite an analytical person. I never expected myself to be a teacher, researcher or author, and I never really deliberately worked towards those paths in life. But they were the exact roles I found myself thrust into as a result of following my inner calling. I enjoy these vocations tremendously, and I derive great satisfaction from them. On the contrary, I have friends who have tried hard to engineer their careers in meticulous ways, through careful and strategic planning of their career paths. Most of them are unhappy with what they have gotten themselves into, although they are right where they planned to be.

Trying to figure out the pathways to get to our goals has never been our job. Instead, our part of the creative equation has always been to decide what we want, and then focus on that final outcome clearly on the inside. This is just a different way of saying "holding a pure intention on the inside." Our job is to focus wholeheartedly on the final desired outcome that we want and then let the Universe present ways or means that will allow for the fulfillment of those desires. The ways and means have never been for us to figure out. This is why people who are trying to take action to "attract" their good are exerting unnecessary effort. We can never figure out what is the right action to take to attract our good. Leave all of that to the Universe and let it guide you. Focus on the first part of the equation.

This is where our inner state comes into the picture. Our inner state is our consciousness and everything that goes on within us at any one time. Since we are always one with the Universe, the Universe picks up on everything that is in our inner state and responds accordingly. If you hold an intention purely in your inner state, that intention goes on to influence energetic matter in the world around you. However, if you also simultaneously hold on to feelings of self-doubt, worry, blame, resentment, guilt and so on, then those feelings will be acted upon by the Universe as well. You will soon see their physical counterparts in the world around you. You will find more circumstances and reasons to doubt, worry, blame, resent, and to feel guilty about—and so on.

Therefore, if the things you have asked for are still not yet in your physical experience, it is **not** because you are not asking hard enough, or because you do not want it badly enough. A very light intention is all that is needed to make something happen in your outer reality. More often than not, it is because your inner state is simultaneously clouded with negative thoughts that contradict your primary intentions. All of these negative thoughts, emotions and feelings represent various forms of resistance to your final manifestations.

The biggest secret hiding in plain view is this: When you drop all (or most) of your resistances on the inside leaving only your desired intentions, then whatever you ask for **must happen** very quickly for you. Manifestations can happen in a matter of minutes, hours or days. But you must first find an effective way to **drop all of your resistance on the inside first**. Only then can the results manifest themselves in your outer reality. This is Universal Law.

My entire quest has been to find more effective techniques to help my readers drop their manifestation resistances. You'll find that I seldom emphasize the "doing" part in my books, instead choosing to focus on the "being" aspect. This is because beingness is key to our outer manifestations. The kind of things that happen in our outer reality is in direct relation to who we are (how we feel) on the inside, as opposed to what we do in terms of physical actions.

Let us explore the usage of affirmations and how they fit into the framework I have discussed above. Many self-help teachers recommend the use of effectively crafted affirmations for the manifestation of our desires. You'll find that the use of the same affirmations has worked wonders for some people while producing no results at all for others. What is the difference here? If you study the cases in which affirmations have worked, you will find that the repetition of certain statements has produced a genuine change in the inner emotional state of these individuals. Through the repetition of certain statements, these individuals have felt more hopeful and have lessened their feelings of fear, worry or doubt. These are the individuals for whom affirmations will work. In other individuals, the repetition of the same statements magnifies and stirs up more negative feelings. The use of affirmations causes them to pay more attention to the disparity between where they currently are and what they are affirming. It is for this latter group that affirmations will not work.

The same happens in the case of visualizations. I have asked many individuals to visualize the exact same visual sequences, and some have produced amazing results while others have produced none. Why the difference? Again, the act of visualization allowed the former group to get in touch with the feelings and emotions associated with the fulfillment of their desires. These feelings, which they would not have accessed during their usual waking hours, sped up the manifestation of their desires. For the latter group, visualizations caused them to feel more desperate and made the *lack* of what they were asking for more apparent.

So, the same practices—but two vastly different outcomes for different people. This means that there is no one-size-fits-all when it comes to manifesting our desires. A customized hybrid approach must be adopted. If you belong to the former group for whom the use of these manifestation techniques creates good feelings, then you should continue with them in moderation. If you belong to the latter group for whom the use of these outer techniques amplifies your feelings of lack, then alternative methods are needed to deal with these persistent negative feelings. Remember that once the negative feelings are dealt with, and once you have restored your inner state to one of peace, your job is done! What you ask for has to materialize in your outer reality very quickly.

CHAPTER THREE

HOW I DISCOVERED THOUGHTLESS MANIFESTATIONS

L ike most people, I tried various ways to let go of the negative feelings that occupied my waking consciousness. In my case, the negative feelings that were the most pervasive were my feelings of worry (worrying over whether my manifestations would come true and how they would materialize), feelings of fear (of not having enough, not getting what I wanted) and feelings of impatience.

Over the years, I have found these to be the top three negative feelings that dominate our inner states. However, because our predominant negative feelings are caused by years of negative conditioning, yours may differ. Some people feel a constant sense of anger or resentment about the world around them, while others may feel guilty about their past. It is a good idea to take note of the major negative feelings (themes) in your life and start paying attention to them. These negative feelings offer a clue as to why your manifestations have been slow in coming.

In my case, I worked on one negative feeling at a time as they came up. Whenever I felt a sense of worry, I would stop and apply the letting-go process described in several of my books. This letting-go process is based on the work of Lester Levenson, creator of the Sedona Method. As I have written before, I have yet to find anything more effective than the Sedona Method when it comes to dropping our long-held negative feelings. As you deal with the feelings that come up in each moment, you lessen their emotional charge and their intensity. Very soon, these feelings will crop up less and less for you. Even when they do, you'll be able to let go of them more easily than ever before.

Notice that I focused my efforts entirely on the dropping of negative feelings that impeded my physical manifestations. This is a key part of the process. I paid little attention to the physical actions I could take to "attract" or to ask for what I wanted. This is because once the obstacles (the predominant negative feelings) along a path have been removed, then what we ask for has to come easily and effortlessly. When you feel calm and peaceful on the inside, any intention held in that consciousness has to come true very easily.

A great epiphany came over me when I read the words of spiritual teacher Dr. David Hawkins in his book "Letting Go." It is interesting to note that Dr. Hawkins was also an early student of the Sedona Method. The book must have been around four hundred pages long but one particular sentence leapt out at me as I read it (and I paraphrase): "Ignore thoughts. They are merely endless rationalizations of inner feelings."

Ignore thoughts.

Something about those two words made my heart race and I felt goosebumps all over my body. Could this be the next piece I was looking for? I read those words again: "**Ignore thoughts**. They are merely endless rationalizations of inner feelings."

And in that moment, I understood.

I realized that each time I felt worried on the inside, worrisome thoughts were going through my mind. Each time I felt fearful on the inside, fearful thoughts played out the various doomsday scenarios in my consciousness. Each time I felt angry about something or someone, my mind chatter was giving me reasons and events to support those angry feelings.

While this may seem obvious, the profoundly simple solution has also been in plain sight all along: To drop all the negative feelings and resistances that block our manifestations—simply **ignore** all thoughts. Leave them out of our manifestations. But is it possible to hold an intention and ask for something without the use of any thoughts?

Contemplating further, I realized that it is indeed possible to ask for something without thinking about it in words. Dr. Hawkins' words ignited completely new possibilities in me and set up new realities which I had not even considered in the past. I realize that I had placed too much emphasis on the use of words, going as far to assume that words were the only means we could invoke the manifestation process. Our use of language for self-expression is so natural to us that words are the first things we automatically turn to when we wish to communicate with the Universe. We use words as a medium to convey our desires in times of prayer, and we use words to state our intentions.

But what if we could do all that *without* the use of words? By dropping the use of words, I realized that I could drop thought. There would be nothing left for me to think about. This was a true breakthrough for me. It was then that I realized the manifestation process could be completely silent and without thought, and I could still manifest (as if by magic!) without uttering a single word or having a single thought in the process.

This is the premise we will be exploring more deeply in the chapters to come. But for now, I would like you to turn inward and pay attention to what is happening in your inner consciousness. Notice how words have become such a fundamental form of communication in your life. Words allow you to think. As you read my words on this page, you are probably repeating these printed words silently to yourself in your mind. At the same time, you are consciously thinking about what you have just read, and these blocks of thought present themselves as strings of words in your mind.

Now let's take this thought experiment a little further. What would happen if you lost your ability to use words to communicate? What would be left for you to communicate with? One quickly realizes that although we have lost our ability to think in terms of words, we can still hold certain feelings in our consciousness. Therefore, you do not need words to allow you to *feel* happy, sad, or angry. The words may make it easier for you to get to those emotional states, but holding that emotional state and holding those thoughts in your mind are two different things.

This is the first fundamental step in applying the art of thought-less manifestations in your life. For the majority of us, thoughts and words are so synonymous with our feelings that we do not realize they can be separated. It is only through some contemplation that we realize our thoughts are not our feelings, and our feelings are not our thoughts. As Dr. David Hawkins rightfully pointed out, our thoughts often provide the **rationalizations** for our feelings. Our thoughts give us reasons to feel a particular way, but they are not a substitute for our feelings.

This is a very powerful understanding to have, because it means that there is an easy way to drop all your resistant negative feelings. You may have previously believed that you could not get rid of your negative feelings of worry, fear or desperation—no matter how hard you tried. The reason why these feelings seemed so persistent in your consciousness is not because of the feelings themselves (which can easily be let go of), but because of the thoughts associated with those feelings. Notice how a myriad of thoughts often accompany our feelings—so much so that we do not know what causes what. Do the thoughts cause us to feel our feelings more intensely, or do the feelings cause us to attract more thoughts? Readers of my books will know that the effect works in both directions. Thoughts cause us to feel more feelings, which is the rationalization aspect as outlined by Dr. David Hawkins. But at the same time, our feelings attract corresponding thoughts. This is the Law of Attraction at work at the most fundamental level.

Why is this realization important? First, it means that you'll be able to get rid of a huge chunk of negative emotions which have been bothering you, simply by paying no attention to their associated thoughts, and focusing only on the feelings. Suppose that you feel a sense of worry as you are going about your daily activities. Probing further, you realize that worrying thoughts are also in your consciousness. You find yourself worrying over how your bills for the month will be paid. Now this is a thought that has to be distinguished from the feeling of worry itself. This is a thought that gives you a reason to worry, **but only if you engage or believe in that thought.** The latter part of the sentence is key: You worry only if you choose to engage in that thought. You are unaffected by the thought (and hence you do not worry) if you choose to disregard it.

Disregarding all thoughts that permeate your consciousness will be difficult in the beginning. The practice seems difficult because we have been so used to having voices in our heads that talk to us and provide some order to our thinking. However, what I am suggesting here is not that you silence all thoughts; that will come later. Instead, I am suggesting that you **ignore** all thought. Let them continue playing in the background, but simply make a conscious decision to ignore them. When you hear your mind chatter saying, "How rude is his response! He always speaks in such a condescending manner to me…" Choose to *disregard* that thought instead of engaging in it. Treat it as false and ignore it. Skip over it. You will find miraculous changes occurring in your outer reality soon afterward if you do this with sufficient regularity over a large number of your thoughts.

"*But what if my thoughts are true?*" Notice how that is just another thought in itself? The point of this mental exercise is not in discerning whether your thoughts are true or otherwise. I am not saying that all your thoughts are false, but there is great value in *treating* and disregarding them *as* false. Why is that so? Recall the manifestation framework which I outlined earlier: Negative feelings, when held in our consciousness over a long period of time with sufficient intensity, go on to create our outer realities. When we remove such negative feelings from our inner state, we remove all blocks that are standing between us and our desired good and hence the manifestations have to happen quickly.

By treating most of your thoughts as false, you are removing the influence these thoughts have on your inner state. Instead of engaging in them, believing in them and intensifying those negative feelings, you nip the problem in the bud. Those thoughts may still replay in your consciousness, but by applying a blanket rule to disregard them (very much like the spam filter in your email program), you prevent these negative messages from even reaching your inbox in the first place. All of those thoughts can replay themselves as much as they like and you would not be the least bit affected by them. Of course, this is just the beginning. As you progress through these exercises and through this book, you will find the unwanted thoughts completely silenced by the end of this book. You will have effectively reached what I call the *thought-less* state, which is a truly manifestative state.

Most people are afraid that disregarding their thoughts will make them unable to function in life. What I am saying here applies only to the frivolous mind chatter that occupies much of our waking consciousness and drains our energy. You'll be surprised at how much more energetic you feel after trying this exercise out for a week. When you stop entertaining every single (false) thought that appears in your consciousness, you free up lots of energy for productive and directed mental activity. The reason why I suggest ignoring **all** thought in the beginning (as opposed to only the negative thoughts) is because your mind chatter will be predominantly and overwhelmingly negative at the start, such that there is little value in manually sifting through your thoughts.

Of course, you always have a choice as to when you would like to flip the quiet switch and move into a thought-less mode. The above steps do not apply when you need your mental faculties for proper work. For instance, when you are evaluating a business proposal or if you're trying to come up with one, that is the time you should entertain and engage in your own thoughts! Knowing when to engage in your thoughts and when to ignore them will be of great value when applying these spiritual principles in your life.

CHAPTER FOUR
THE BASICS OF THOUGHT-LESS MANIFESTATIONS

In the previous chapter, I shared the powerful practice of ignoring all your extraneous thoughts and dealing only with the feelings that crop up for you in each moment. You will find that when you use the letting go process on only the feelings themselves but not the distracting thoughts, the work gets done sooner and faster. You will find it easier to restore your inner state to one of calmness and peace.

It will not be easy to ignore all your thoughts, especially in the beginning. The main purpose of the preceding exercise was to allow you to recognize the difference between your thoughts and your feelings. Your thoughts are not your feelings, but merely serve to amplify and perpetuate whatever you are feeling in the moment. As you make a conscious decision to ignore all your extraneous thoughts, you realize how much of your negative feelings were actually perpetuated by those uncontrolled thoughts. When you ignore the mind chatter as a result of those extraneous thoughts, you gradually free yourself from the influence of your past programming.

In this chapter, I am going to share a powerful method to hold an intention in your consciousness *without* the use of thoughts or words. This forms the basis of thought-less manifestations. All of what I have written in Chapter 2 about the manifestation framework still applies, except that now we are going to repeat the whole process without the use of any words. While it may seem difficult or strange in the beginning, stick with me and the process will become second nature to you in due course. You'll realize the speed and efficacy of this new thought-less method as compared to what you have achieved previously through the use of cumbersome words.

In order for us to transition to a completely thought-less state, it is necessary for us to first use some words and thoughts to get there. I have often encouraged the use of outcome statements to identify and clarify what we want. An outcome statement is one that states clearly and succinctly, in as few words as possible, the end result or final outcome that you would like to manifest. For example, if you would like to manifest more financial abundance in your life, then your intention can be stated as: "I intend financial abundance" or "I feel peaceful about my finances."

An outcome statement can also be used in direct response to a perceived problem or issue. By stating an outcome statement in response to an undesired situation, there is no need to describe what the problem is. For example, if you are currently facing financial debt (the problem you are trying to eliminate), there is no need to say, "I intend $1,000 in extra income each month to pay off my debt." Phrasing your outcome statement in this way simultaneously brings up the very problem you are trying to eliminate (the debt itself), and also insists that the solution comes through a specific path (through an additional thousand dollars every month). The Universe has infinite ways to make things happen in your life and always knows the most direct pathways to what you are asking for. By insisting that things happen through a particular logical path, you are closing yourself off to other possibilities and limiting your options.

It is worth spending some time to fine-tune your outcome statements until they clearly state your desired end result. An ideal outcome statement is one which (1) does not bring to mind the undesired situation you are trying to change, (2) does not dictate that things happen in a particular way, and (3) uses as few words as possible. When you state your desired outcome in only a few words, you reduce the chances of generating extraneous thoughts and negative feelings about the situation.

The purpose of an outcome statement is to give us an internal representation of how we would like the ideal situation to be like. There is always a natural tendency to focus on the undesirable situation at hand—and as long as we do, it will be difficult for our current reality to change. Our continued focus on an undesirable situation, no matter what it may be, causes more thought energy to flow toward that situation, thus perpetuating its existence. This is why thinking about, worrying about and even talking about your various problems in life in an attempt to find solutions for them actually achieves the exact opposite! You may think that you are focusing on the solution, but you are actually channeling the energy in the *opposite* direction—toward the problem itself!

A well-crafted outcome statement takes a very light touch and does not automatically bring to mind the undesirable situation (the problem) which we are trying to eliminate. When you craft a proper outcome statement, the perceived problem is already half solved. Hence there is no need to rush through this process. Ensure that you have a clear picture of the final outcome in your mind. I have found that whenever manifestations were slow in coming for me, it was often because I did not have a clear outcome in my mind. My outcome statement was either scattered in its focus (trying to achieve too many things at once) or focused on the wrong aspects of the situation. When I fine-tuned my outcome statement to get right to the heart-of-the-matter, the physical manifestations showed up very quickly.

A well-crafted outcome statement focuses your thought energy on the *solution* as opposed to the problem. Again, there is a very subtle difference between focusing on the lack of your manifestations, as opposed to the presence of your manifestations. Many people think they are focusing on the presence of their manifestations, when in fact they are focusing on the lack. Therefore, a well-crafted out-come statement helps us direct our energies towards a more desired reality. The moment we reduce our fixation on the current undesired reality by focusing on a more desired reality, the current reality straightens itself out because we are no longer perpetuating its existence through our consciousness.

After you have crafted your outcome statement, hold that intention in your awareness. Notice how that intention makes you feel. It should make you feel a sense of lightness, peace or joy. If you intend for abundance, you should then feel a corresponding sense of abundance. If you are asking for perfect health, then you should feel the sense of well-being that comes with having optimal health. Now this is a very important aspect of the thought-less manifestations process—notice how you used the words contained in the outcome statement to get to your current inner state. You are not holding the words themselves in your consciousness, but you are holding particular *feelings* and *emotions* associated with your intention. Do not proceed until you are aware of the difference between the mere words used in your outcome statement, and the feelings which they evoke within you.

We often mistake our outcome statements with our intentions. We may repeat the underlying words that make up our intentions, and over time, come to believe that the words form our intentions. This is not true. There is a distinction between the words used to express our intentions, and the very intentions themselves. Become especially aware of this subtle difference as you turn inwards.

To do so, it may be helpful to sit in a comfortable spot and close your eyes. Turn your conscious awareness inwards and perceive with your inner senses. Next, select one outcome statement which you would like to use for this exercise and hold it purely in your conscious awareness. Notice that in order to hold the intention in your consciousness, you had to use certain words to get there. These are the words that make up your outcome statement. These words may be something like, "I intend abundance" or "I intend peace." But the mere words themselves are not your intentions. Your intentions are not the words which you just repeated silently to yourself. If so, what is the nature of your intention?

Ask yourself this question as you sit in quiet contemplation: *"If my intentions are not the words I use to describe them, then what are my intentions made up of?"* Hold this thought in your mind and just allow yourself to sit in the stillness of it all. This is a profound moment, for you are on the brink of an exciting realization. For the first time in your life (and aided along by the exercise in the previous chapter), you realize that you are not your thoughts. Similarly, your intentions are not the words used to describe them. Notice how the words merely helped you to convey what you wanted to intend—and even then, words have often been inadequate for that purpose!

As you sit in stillness and allow this realization to well up within you, notice the **thought-less,** wordless and timeless nature of your intentions. Your intentions just *are*. They are not the words you use to state or describe them. While you had to use words to clearly convey your intentions and help you get into that inner feeling place, words and thoughts are no longer necessary once you become one with that intention. When you merge with the vibrational essence of your intentions and desires, then no words are necessary.

I encourage you to work with one intention at a time. There may be a palpable sense of excitement as you learn these truths and an urgency to work on all your intentions in quick succession, one after another. But I have found that it is best to take a measured approach. Work with one dominant intention in each session, or during a particular phase of your life. You can always move on to the next intention after you are done with the previous one. Pick an intention that is important for you and in alignment with your highest desires. Then notice how you naturally repeat those words to create particular feelings within yourself that represent the intention. Also notice how you stop focusing on the words once you have encapsulated the essence of that intention in your being.

What I would like you to try next is to skip the use of words and thoughts completely. This will be an exciting breakthrough for you. Is it possible to state an intention directly in your inner consciousness **without** using any words or thoughts to get there? Can you hold an intention in your consciousness directly, **bypassing** the use of any physical words? This will take some getting used to in the beginning, but it is a fundamental skill for the thought-less manifestations process.

Initially, you may feel slightly lost as you wonder how to bridge the gap that was previously filled in by those words. If it is difficult for you to hold an intention directly in the beginning, then repeat the outcome / intention statement quietly to yourself, then drop your focus on those words immediately after you have encapsulated the essence of that intention within you. Use the words to help you get there, but once you are there, withdraw your focus from the words themselves. Do not keep repeating the words over and over again in your awareness.

As you become more proficient at this practice, you will be able to jump directly to the feelings themselves. Notice how your body experiences a unique blend of sensations when you hold an intention within you. This unique vibrational signature is the purest essence of an intention, untainted by physical words or extraneous thoughts. This is as pure as an intention can be. Because there are no unnecessary thoughts or words to cloud your awareness, there are no obstacles or blocks that stand in the way of your manifestations. This is the essence of and the first step to thought-less manifestations, where things happen for you the moment you hold an intention in your consciousness without the use of any accompanying thoughts or words.

CHAPTER FIVE

STRENGTHENING THE NON-VERBAL ESSENCE OF YOUR INTENTIONS

Congratulations! You've just had your very first taste of the thought-less manifestations process in the previous chapter. In the following pages, we will talk about how to strengthen the essence of your intentions and apply the technique to a broad variety of everyday situations. You'll be surprised at the new possibilities that emerge for you once you convert most of your verbal intentions into non-verbal and thought-less ones. When you isolate your intentions from all the usual extraneous counter-intentions and worrisome thoughts, the speed at which these inner desires go on to affect your outer reality will be astonishing. You will find your intentions coming true with very little physical effort on your part, apart from the effort it takes to remain focused on your intentions on the inside.

There is a tendency to revert to the use of words, especially in the beginning. I had a difficult time dropping my habit of using words and thoughts to represent my intentions, for language has become a large part of my life. I am sure it is an integral part of yours too. In our society, children are taught to communicate and think in words from a young age, so much so that a non-verbal and wordless way of living becomes unimaginable for us! We have become so dependent on our use of language that we do not realize the inherent limitations imposed by it. For example, there are many feelings and sensations which cannot be accurately described in words. There are cultures in the world that do not have the equivalent words to convey certain ideas and archetypes that we have become so familiar with in the English-speaking world.

A fascinating experiment was conducted with members of the Himba tribe in Namibia, South Africa. The tribe members speak a language that has no word for the color blue. During the experiment, tribe members had a difficult time picking out blue colored squares from green colored squares. While this task would have been simple even for our preschool children, tribe members could not distinguish between the two colors because they have never been conditioned to differentiate them through their language!

Of course, I am not suggesting that we eschew the use of words completely. Words are a necessary and useful tool when it comes to outer communications. If I wanted to convey my ideas succinctly to you, my best bet would still be in the form of the written or spoken word, rather than just sitting quietly in silence and hoping that my thoughts will be transmitted to you. Incidentally, such non-verbal thought transmittance has been found to be common in many ancient spiritual cultures (most notably the Tibetan culture), implying that possibilities certainly exist should we choose to go beyond the written word! But for now, the conveyance of these ideas from me to you still has to be made via the written words on this page.

Words become a limitation when we cling to them and see them as the only way to represent our intentions. You'll quickly find that words are wholly inadequate to represent our rich inner states and feelings. Yet most people force things to happen through the use of endless mantras, affirmations, prayers and invocations. One has to realize that there is no inherent power in the mere words used. The power always comes from the unique sensations and feelings that the words evoke within ourselves. And here's an even more powerful concept that forms the gist of this book: **You do not need words to evoke these powerful feelings within yourself.** You can completely drop your use of words and still hold the same intention non-verbally, within your consciousness.

There are several advantages to holding thought-less and non-verbal intentions. One major advantage is that you drop a whole lot of negative fears, worries and unnecessary distracting thoughts (collectively referred to as "resistances") which impede your outer manifestations. Because we have become so used to believing in and associating with our thoughts, our intentions usually bring up associated mind chatter, which in turn brings about more related thoughts. For example, thinking of the simple intention of "I intend an income of $10,000 a month" may simultaneously bring up negative thoughts related to self-worth and deservingness. Some of the unresourceful yet associated thoughts may include: "*Who do you think you are to deserve such an income? Your parents didn't make that much! No one in your family makes that much! What will your friends think of you? There are many more talented people out there who don't make that kind of money...*" You get the idea. Our inner critic is often caustic and unkind. But where do all these ugly thoughts come from? They come from our negative storehouse of unconscious beliefs and memories which we have picked up along the way.

If you follow the traditional method of stating your intentions in words, then you also have to deal with all these self-defeating and discouraging thoughts that automatically come up. Each intention may bring about a whole string of self-defeating thoughts, which in turn produce more negative feelings of disappointment, fear and self-doubt. This is the reason why it can be difficult for people to manifest their desires in the beginning. The overwhelmingly negative social conditioning which they have received gives rise to overwhelmingly negative self-talk, which muddies their inner states even more and prevents them from holding a singular, pure intention.

Before I discovered this non-verbal process, I advocated the dropping (letting go) of these negative feelings. This worked well to produce miraculous results in my life. I have since discovered that combining the letting-go process with these non-verbal protocols results in speedier and more effective manifestations, every single time. The non-verbal method works because by disregarding and ignoring all of our extraneous thoughts, we allow ourselves to focus singularly on our desired intentions, one at a time. The speed and precision of your outer manifestations always depends on how purely you hold an intention in your inner state to the exclusion of everything else. "Everything else" in this case means your negative thoughts and feelings.

On the other hand, the letting-go process (which is taught in my other books) works because it removes the negative emotional charge associated with our negative feelings. When we let go of all the negative feelings in our consciousness, we return to a pure and calm inner state that is conducive to our outer manifestations. Therefore, the letting-go process helps to create a blank canvas for our intentions, while the non-verbal process covered in this book helps us to focus more purely and intently on our desires.

Think of your inner state as a blank, pristine canvas on which your brush strokes are made. The canvas represents your inner state, which has to be as pure and undisturbed as possible. After all, who would want to paint on a used canvas? The painting on the canvas represents your intentions. Suppose that you would like to paint a circle. This circle represents your primary intention. It wouldn't help if your circle is simultaneously painted over and obscured by many other erratic brush strokes. Who would know you are painting a circle in that case? These erratic brush strokes represent our negative feelings and extraneous thoughts which we are seeking to drop. These unnecessary strokes obscure the original idea which we are trying to convey—the circle itself. Finally—and this is the key—the paint brush, brush stroke and paint which we use represent the methods, thoughts and words used to express our intentions. The paint brush or even the paint itself (thoughts and words) help us paint that perfect circle onto the canvas, but **they are not the circle**. The circle is not the paint which we used to draw it.

Most people have no trouble understanding this analogy. They'll say, "Of course the circle is not the paint. The paint is only used to draw the circle but nothing more." This is the same idea which I'm trying to convey in this book. The words which you use to represent your intentions are not the intentions themselves. Your intentions are an energetic creation which arose from your own beingness. The words you use merely help to express, represent and communicate them.

I was not bound by any expectations when I first started on this journey. Since I did not know what to expect or what was possible, I embarked upon this new journey with an open mind. I decided to see if non-verbal ways of holding my intentions were possible, but I did not always succeed in the beginning. More often than not, I found myself reverting to the use of words and language to express my intentions. But that was alright. What mattered was that I made a conscious decision to reduce my reliance on language and on physical words. I decided to experiment with holding an intention directly without the use of any physical words. While it felt strange in the beginning, and while I still depended largely on words and thoughts to guide my experience, I was soon able to eschew my use of words completely.

In the same way, there is no pressure when applying any of this. You do not have to give up your use of words completely when representing your intentions. What I would suggest that you do is to start with the steps we covered previously.

First, make a conscious decision to ignore all thought. This will be a great starting point and an epiphany for you. As you manage to successfully ignore *some* of your thoughts, you will realize that **you are not your thoughts**. You are not your feelings. You have merely been using your thoughts to represent and justify how you feel. But your thoughts are not even a part of you. They are false projections and creations of your ego mind. When you reduce this reliance on your own thoughts, you start to see how you have always existed independently and separately from your thoughts. You are still whole, complete and alive without your thoughts! This is such a liberating "thought" in itself, which makes you feel upbeat and joyful. But it is also a thought, so how about ignoring this thought as well…and so on?

As you stick firmly to your decision of completely ignoring all thought, you'll find that much of the undesired physical circumstances that are in your current reality are propped up by nothing but your own sustained negative thoughts (beliefs) about the situation! You'll realize that physical reality is perpetuated in large part because of your unresourceful and self-defeating thoughts. By dropping and ignoring these thoughts as they arise, you'll find many of the undesirable situations in your life dropping away in one fell swoop.

People who used to upset you no longer enter into your daily life because you no longer hold them there psychically. Unfavorable circumstances dissolve of their own accord because you are no longer fixated on them, nor perpetuating them on the inside. Even physical healings manifest themselves once you let go of your extraneous and fearful thoughts surrounding your physical conditions. As I write in my book "Manifestation Pathways," my own encounter with knee pain was largely perpetuated by my own fearful and misconceived thoughts about the situation. I had inadvertently bought into these false thoughts, and even made changes to the way I moved about in order to accommodate my anticipated pain. While the physical pain I felt back then was certainly real, most of the distress came from worrying about the pain and the "hopelessness" of the situation. Once I was able to isolate and drop all the unresourceful negative thoughts, a pathway for healing spontaneously presented itself.

While one may hold strong intentions for a particular desired outcome, they may also unconsciously sabotage themself by holding onto many unresourceful beliefs and thoughts about the situation. For example, a natural intention that arises when one suffers from a physical condition is for healing to occur. This is the primary intention. Yet at the same time, healing cannot occur if the individual holds many counter-intentions, or negative thoughts and feelings in their consciousness. For example, if they spend a large part of their time worrying about the supposed "incurability" of their condition or feeling discouraged as a result of their situation, then all of these will prevent their primary intention for healing to be held purely in their consciousness.

It is the same for any other intention which you may hold in your consciousness, be it for tangible objects or for intangible experiences. While your desire for what you're asking for may be very intense, you cannot simultaneously hold that primary intention while still allowing yourself to be swayed by extraneous thoughts. This is why ignoring all thoughts is a great first step. It helps to restore your inner state to one of calmness and peace such that you focus on your primary intentions to the exclusion of everything else. When you manage to do so even for short periods of time, the results have to show up as physical manifestations in your outer reality.

CHAPTER SIX

WHAT DOES AN INTENTION FEEL LIKE?

Each intention has its own unique vibrational signature. This unique blend of inner sensations becomes more apparent to you once you ignore all thoughts and drop your use of words to describe how you feel on the inside.

There are really two parts to the thought-less manifestations process. The first part is to drop the use of words when holding your intentions. Instead of repeating an intention statement or describing a desired outcome quietly to yourself in order to feel a particular way (for example, "My credit application is now approved"), eschew your use of words completely and go directly to the feelings themselves. *Feel*—for how it would feel within yourself if you expressed that intention in feelings instead of words. What would it feel like for you? How would that intention feel for you if it is true, right now, in this very moment? What is the vibrational essence of that intention?

Avoid the natural tendency to use words to describe your feelings. Remember that anytime you do so, you place self-imposed labels on your feelings that unconsciously limit the broad range of feelings that is possible in any moment.

You may find it easier to do this exercise with your eyes closed. In the beginning, no feelings may come to you as you find it somewhat difficult or unnatural to express your intention clearly without the use of words. But just let everything be alright. Close your eyes and focus on the deep feeling of inner peace within. Then allow yourself to slowly feel the vibrational essence of that desire without the use of any words. If any words or thoughts come to your mind, gently let them go. Ignore them. Do not engage in them. Take a light touch and just focus on feeling your intentions within.

You will soon notice two things. You'll feel a deep, pure feeling of (what can be best described as) a sense of positive expectancy. Notice how I am limited by my use of words here, but this is the closest physical description that I can come up with. This feeling of positive expectancy—like that of lightly wanting something to happen—is your feeling of *intent.* Notice how focused and pure this feeling is without the presence of any extraneous descriptive words or thoughts. Notice how you are, quite possibly for the first time in your life, feeling the vibrational essence of this intention purely without the use of any words or qualifiers to describe your experience. This is as pure as an intention can get.

The second part of the thought-less manifestations process is to avoid using any words to describe your experience. You may immediately be tempted to place descriptive labels on these feelings once you have felt them. They may feel like joy, or expectancy, or a sense of lightness and peace to you. But resist the urge to use words to describe how you are feeling on the inside. The reason is that words bring about associative thoughts, which will once again clutter our inner states with more and more unnecessary associated thoughts. So just immerse yourself in that experience. Instead, ask yourself non-verbally how you can strengthen that feeling. How can you make that feeling stronger? How can you feel more of it, more intently? What you are doing here is something very powerful. You are holding the vibrational essence of your desire in its purest, intentional form, unadulterated by any extraneous thoughts or the use of descriptive words. You are experiencing the fullness of your experience because you are not placing any limits on your own experience. You are perceiving everything as it is, free from the filters typically created by your own distracting thoughts.

This is how an intention feels for you in its purest form. Play with this for a moment and practice *feeling* different intentions in their purest form. First decide which intention you would like to work with. Then hold that intention in your consciousness, going directly to the feelings themselves *without* the use of any physical words. Once you have felt the vibrational essence of the intention clearly in your consciousness, see if you can lightly hold it there without describing the experience or placing any descriptive labels on it. You may notice yourself saying, "*This feels so good! I feel so happy that I feel so good!*" If so, gently ignore that thought. Ignore all thoughts that come up in your mind. Focus on the *feelings* associated with the intention.

Once you have identified what the purest nonverbal feeling of your intention feels like, see if you can strengthen that feeling in your conscious awareness. Again, you do not have to deliberately conjure up any of that feeling in order to turn up its intensity. All you have to do is to become more aware of it. Have you ever had music playing in the background while you worked at some other task? When you were absorbed in your task, the music playing in the background became barely audible. However, once you decided to pay conscious attention to the music playing in the background, it was as if someone suddenly turned up the volume. The same applies here. You are not trying to turn up the volume of the music, but rather, to become more aware of the feelings that are already there. By quieting yourself and adopting the stance of a neutral observer, you notice how that intention feels for you. You begin to notice more and more of that intention and its nuances in your inner state.

The feeling of positive expectancy feels right and joyous in every way. When you hold your intentions purely in your consciousness, you should not feel a sense of strain or struggle. The whole experience should feel effortless for you. If you feel even the slightest strain or discomfort, it means that you are trying too hard. Perhaps you may be trying to conjure up the feelings artificially, or you may be engaged in the exercise with the mindset of forcing something to happen. Let all of that go and just enjoy the exercise for what it is. This is not an exercise to make anything happen on the outside. It is not a technique to make anything come true. Instead, this is a process where we experience our purest connections with Universal source energy and recognize the connection that has always been there.

There is no need to tense any part of your body or attempt to "broadcast" your intention in any way as part of this exercise. As mentioned, we are not trying to make anything happen on the outside. All we are doing is getting in touch with how an intention feels non-verbally for us on the inside. Getting in touch with these feelings is important, because two things are happening simultaneously when you get to that place of pure, positive energy. First, you are holding onto that intention very purely and powerfully in the total absence of any resistant thoughts or feelings. By virtue of these Universal Laws, it means that your intention has to manifest very quickly in your outer reality! Second, you are recognizing and affirming how this intention feels to you. Most people go through life without ever *feeling* the true essence of their intentions! No wonder their intentions do not come true for them; because they have neither held these intentions clearly on the inside, nor identified with them.

We may *think* we are asking for a particular outcome, but the vibrational essence of what we feel on a regular basis may be vastly different. In my book "Banned Money Secrets" which talks about the manifestation of money using spiritual principles, I encourage readers to get in touch with their feelings of abundance. One of my readers later wrote that she had a difficult time feeling abundant. That was when she realized she had never identified what abundance truly felt like for her. In the same way, we may *think* we are asking for abundance, when in fact we may be asking for something else, by virtue of the feelings which we hold on the inside!

In order to start the manifestation process, we first have to formulate and hold an intention on the inside. This intention is the spark which starts everything off. In "Banned Manifestation Secrets," I talk about how there is no fixed way to state an intention. Some people may find it more effective to state their intentions in actions instead of words. We are now going through a much more effective way to state your intentions by skipping the use of words completely. But the point still remains that you *have* to state your intentions in the first place! You cannot accurately state your intentions if you have not identified with how they feel for you on the inside.

When you get to that place of no thoughts, no words and just pure feelings, your job is done. There is nothing else you have to do. This becomes easier with practice and some persistence. When I first started having fun with this method, I did not know what to expect. I was not guided by any expectations or prior experience. So I just focused on seeing how far I could go with this method. I would try to hold an intention on the inside without the use of any words and curiously observe what would subsequently happen on the outside. Sometimes the feelings representing the intention would come to me easily and stay there. At other times, it took a little bit longer before those feelings began to show up for me. Shortly after, I could go directly to the vibrational essence of the intentions themselves without any words and stay there. That was when more magic and miracles started happening for me!

The whole process takes no more than a few seconds for me nowadays. If I had to quantify the entire process, I would say that it takes around two to three seconds for me to feel an intention strongly on the inside using the non-verbal method, and to get to that place free from any extraneous words or thoughts. Once I am there, I remain for a few more seconds (usually five to eight) while I immerse myself fully in the purest vibrational essence of my desires. I do so until I feel everything "click" into place on the inside. That's when I know that *it is done.* I come out of my relaxed, yet focused state and resume my daily activities (or go right to sleep, if it is the last thing I do before bed).

I am providing these numbers here for your reference, mainly to show that the process does not take long and that you do not have to stay in a thought-less, focused state for inordinate amounts of time. However, each person is different and you should not rush through the process. Take as much time as is needed for yourself.

Once you get to that place on the inside where there are no thoughts and no words but just the purest feelings representing your intentions…there is no need to stay there for long. You will know when you get to that inner sanctuary because everything seems to fall in place and "click" together on the inside. That is when you know you have clearly stated your intention, and that there is nothing more you need to do.

You have just made an imprint and started a ripple in the Universal energy field, which will now go on to attract the outer circumstances and people needed for the fulfillment of your desires. There is nothing else you have to do, for it is truly done on your behalf! If there is anything more you need to do, the next step will be shown to you clearly. You will be led to outer actions which you need to take in the form of inner nudges and inspirations.

One of the earliest spiritual lessons I learned still applies here: Resist the urge to "check reality" once you try a particular technique. There is a tendency for many to check and see if outer circumstances have changed immediately after trying a particular technique, process or method. This would be displaying a lack of faith in these Universal Laws. Know that the moment you ask, it is done. Everything comes in its own divine timing and in its own divine way, so there is no need for you to constantly check to see if the things you asked for have arrived. The postman will ring the bell when he is at the door, and you will not miss it! Besides, we are only aware of an extremely small slice of reality at any one time— so we can never really be sure which aspect of reality has changed! Change may have already occurred in the spectrum that is beyond our perceptual abilities.

Instead, just do your inner work. Focus on holding your intentions purely and getting to that inner place completely absent from any extraneous words or thoughts. Feel the purest vibrational essence of your desires. When you get to that place, you are done! Give thanks that you are done and rest in the peacefulness of it all. What are you done with? You have done your part in the Universal equation and now is the time for the Universe to respond accordingly. It always does.

CHAPTER SEVEN

INTRODUCTION TO NON-VERBAL PROTOCOLS

Congratulations! I know this is the second time I have congratulated you in this book, but you have reached yet another important milestone. In the chapters that follow, we will discuss specific applications and uses of the thoughtless manifestations method, including how you can use them to help others. I call these specific applications "non-verbal protocols," because they involve a series of steps and shortcuts that will stretch the boundaries of what's possible in your own life.

Please note that these protocols are merely suggestions and starting points for you to create your own miracles. They are not cast in stone, nor are they meant to be prescriptive steps that shouldn't ever be deviated from. I am sharing a few of my favorite protocols here because they have worked beautifully to create changes in my own life, and I believe they will be beneficial to you too, as you explore the process. Feel free to adapt the protocols in any way you see fit to create even more magic, miracles and manifestations for yourself and others.

To understand the use of these non-verbal protocols, let's first start with the **basic recipe** covered in the first half of this book. As you will be familiar by now, the basic recipe consists of three steps: First, you decide on the intention (final outcome) which you want. Second, you focus on that intention in a non-verbal and thought-less manner, going directly to the feelings associated with the intention. Third, once you reach that place of pure feeling and the absence of any words or thoughts on the inside, you hold the feeling / intention for a few more seconds until you receive an inner confirmation.

Different people may sense this inner confirmation in different ways. For example, I often feel a sense of profound peacefulness and calm wash over me, and I know intuitively that there is nothing more I have to do about a situation. This is often described in spiritual texts as "a peace which surpasses all understanding." Others may feel things clicking into place on the inside and perceive a sense of closure or settlement. Note that this feeling of inner confirmation is independent of external events or physical circumstances. It is not dependent on anything happening on the outside. It is the Universe's way of letting us know that our affairs are in order, and that things are now happening in direct response to our intentions.

Once you receive an inner confirmation, you can gently come out of an inner-focused state and resume your daily activities.

The three steps described above form the basics of the thought-less manifestations process. Any specific applications will thus be a variation of this basic recipe. For the ease of discussion, these non-verbal protocols can be broadly classified into two groups: protocols that are used on ourselves, and those that are used to help others. I recommend that you become acquainted with the process by using these protocols on yourself first before attempting to help others. As you become more proficient at the process, you'll soon realize that there is really no difference between the two. All perceived separation happens at the level of our ego. In other words, we are all made up of one Universal mind. We are all in this together.

Another helpful tip is to try these protocols in a playful and childlike manner. The more you *play* with this process in a non-expectant manner, the easier it will be for you to create results and changes from the process. I have noted the same thing happening over and over again for energy healers. The more they tried to "influence" or "direct" the healing, the less the desired healing occurred. When they were open to all possibilities, miracles manifested beautifully before their eyes. Therefore, this is not about hard work or effort. If you find yourself straining to apply this material, you are trying too hard! Let go of the outcome and just play with this stuff. Be lighthearted and playful about it.

Remember that we are not using these non-verbal protocols to "make anything happen." Anytime you tell yourself that something *has* to happen, or that you *have* to meet a particular deadline, you are adding unnecessary pressure on yourself. Let all of that go and just have fun with this stuff, just like how you would have fun at the amusement park. Do you go to the amusement park in order to "get something done"? Do you go saying, "I *must* have some fun today! I must! My enjoyment depends on the amount of fun I'll have, so I must have it!" That would be ridiculous. You go to the amusement park knowing that you would already have a fun time no matter what. Similarly, use these processes *knowing* that changes will occur no matter what. Some of the changes that happen may not be immediately perceivable by your physical senses, but that does not mean that changes have not occurred. This is an important realization to make.

Many years ago, I used to read a particular book or try a particular technique and then immediately look to my outer circumstances for evidence of improvement. Of course, I had not yet understood these Universal Laws back then, and I was frequently disappointed. I expected that what I tried would take immediate effect, yet my outer reality seemed to remain the same! I later learned that when nothing seems to shift in our outer reality, it does not mean that change is not happening. Far from that; subtle changes *are* occurring beneath the surface of our everyday reality that are not perceivable to our human senses. I say this not as a way of making you feel better, but because I *know* this to be the true nature of our reality.

For example, when we read a book written by a spiritual master with an elevated consciousness, our own consciousness becomes uplifted by the words of this great master as well. The same thing happens when we simply sit in the presence of a great master with elevated consciousness. Deep changes are occurring in our consciousness at levels which we cannot humanly perceive, yet these transformations are happening in undeniable ways.

While I did not have the chance to personally meet with Lester Levenson—creator of the Sedona Method and whose work I am fond of—those who knew him personally said that he had an endearing personality that drew others to him. People just loved to hang out around him. The same is true for any of the modern day spiritual teachers. They each have a magnetic aura which draws people to them. When you open yourself up and interact with others on an unconditional basis with no expectations, people can sense your absence of motives and open themselves up to you, as well.

There have been instances where I found subtle changes occurring *after* I had gone through a certain course. For example, I once attended Dr. Hew Len's Ho'oponopono training. Ho'oponopono is a Hawaiian spiritual healing practice. I sat through the course as a passive member of the audience without asking any questions, but the real changes occurred afterward. For a few weeks following the course, I noticed a sense of lightness in my perception which I could not explain. It was as if things around me became brighter, or my eyes had somehow let in more light. I also felt a buzzing sensation run through me as I went about my day, which I could pick up as subtle vibrations. Apart from these perceivable changes, I did not notice anything extraordinary and simply went about my daily life. Everything reverted back to normal shortly afterward. I am certain that deeper changes were occurring at that time, which altered the course of my life; I was merely perceiving a very small slice of what was going on back then.

Similarly, I have read wonderful spiritual books only to set them aside after reading and completely forget about their messages. Years later, what I have read in one of those books will spontaneously flash across my mind, while I have the sudden realization that deep changes have indeed occurred in my life without my conscious direction. Somehow, improvements have been made simply by reading the book and *allowing* whatever followed to be alright. This allowing state is important for miracles to occur. We must remain open to all possibilities and know that life is always taking us in the direction of our greatest good.

The most satisfying realization is to notice that something which you have asked for in the past (which you have long forgotten about) has already come true for you. I can't tell you how many times I have walked right into my desired realities without realizing that I asked for them a while back. It would sometimes take me weeks before I realized, "Hey, this is exactly what I asked for! It is now true in my physical reality!"

One good analogy is learning a new language as a child. Do you remember ever picking up a book that was too advanced for your understanding at the time? The words on the pages would have looked like gibberish to you. So you set that book aside, forgot about it and went about your learning of the language. One day, when you picked the book up again, you were pleasantly surprised to find that what you previously thought was gibberish suddenly became completely comprehensible! A whole new world emerged for you through your new level of understanding. Did you make a conscious decision to learn the language so you could read the book? No, you forgot about the book shortly after you put it down. But you allowed your learning to take its course and direct you to all the resources necessary in order for you to achieve mastery in the language. In much the same way, there is no need to deliberately learn this or that technique in order to attract particular circumstances on the outside. All you need to do is follow the basic steps outlined in this book and let your learning take its course. Deep changes are happening—whether you realize it or not.

Sometimes, the changes that we so desperately want to make may not be the best for us. I have written about this several times in the past. There were times when I felt like saying to the Universe, "Just give me X and I'll be happy and stop asking!" But the Universe doesn't work in this manner. It always gives you the true vibrational essence of what you ask for. Therefore, if you ask with lots of forcefulness and desperation, then you're going to get more things to be desperate about, not more of X. You may think you are asking for X, when in fact you are asking for Y. Similarly, you may think that having X will solve all the problems in your life once and for all, but that is only from our limited human understanding of the situation. Things may look very different from a Universal perspective.

So how do we proceed without knowing the full Universal perspective? It's simple. First do your part and then let the Universe lead you to your highest good. The Universe is always nudging you in the direction of your greatest good. Use these non-verbal protocols to state your intention for what you want, and then let go completely. That's why the thought-less manifestations process consists of only three steps, and nothing beyond that. You hold your intention purely and let go completely. Nothing else is needed on your part! From here the Universe takes over and brings you the resources which you need to reach that desired state. It may happen in the way you have foreseen, but oftentimes it does not. There are always more elegant routes to our desired outcomes that we cannot even logically foresee. Through the thought-less manifestations process, we allow ourselves to be led along these infinite pathways to endless possibilities.

Chapter Eight

How to Use Non-Verbal Protocols for Manifestation

In the pages that follow and for the ease of exposition, I will represent each non-verbal protocol as a short phrase and an abbreviation. For example, the non-verbal protocol for directed problem-solving which you will learn about in the next chapter is **solutions space (SS)**. The abbreviation of this protocol is **SS**. There are specific non-verbal protocols to be used for the manifestation of various circumstances and outcomes.

The purpose of these non-verbal protocols is to allow you to quickly and easily **go directly to the feelings themselves** without having to hunt for the right non-verbal representation of an intention or intended outcome. When you use a pre-defined, non-verbal protocol for a particular situation, you immediately hold a very specific and pointed intention designed to invoke that particular outcome. This saves you from the time and effort needed to hunt for the right intention to use in a situation.

I have done much of the work for you by choosing the appropriate non-verbal protocols to be applied in each case. Once again, these are suggestions rather than rules. Think of non-verbal protocols as a memory card loaded with a specific program written for a certain purpose. When you want to work on your spreadsheet, you insert the memory card that contains the spreadsheet program. When you feel like having some fun, you insert the memory card loaded with a game. Similarly, when you want to solve certain issues and manifest specific circumstances in your life, you "load" the non-verbal protocol containing the right intention for that purpose. This saves you from trying a bunch of intentions to see what works, or from having scattered and poorly-formed intentions.

The way you "load" a non-verbal protocol into your consciousness is simple. Recall that the thought-less manifestations process consists of three steps. Step one is where you decide on the intention (final outcome) which you want. In this step, you choose the non-verbal protocol that you would like to use depending on your situation.

Step two is where you go directly to the feelings themselves and hold that intention in your inner consciousness. Along with a description of the non-verbal protocol, I also offer guidance on the feelings associated with each protocol. For example, if you are faced with negative fears and worries about your finances, you would directly apply the **Peace About My Finances (PAMF)** protocol and go straight to strengthening that intention, without having to search for the right intention to use.

Step three of the process remains the same. You hold that intention until a feeling of inner confirmation arises on the inside, at which point you can resume your day's activities.

The abbreviation of the non-verbal protocol, for example **PAMF** or **SS**, comes in handy when you want to feel the feelings associated with that intention purely without the use of any extraneous thoughts or words. Therefore, once you are familiar with a particular protocol, you can simply invoke that feeling on the inside by using its abbreviation rather than the phrase itself. You can simply think **PAMF** on the inside, and instantly be able to hold an intention for peace about your finances.

Chapter Nine

Non-Verbal Protocols for Directed Problem-Solving

I used to think that problems were part-and-parcel of everyday life. For a while, I was even proud of my resourcefulness and problem-solving abilities; the ability to put out one fire after another. It was only after I started studying these spiritual laws that I realized the fallacies in my own thinking and what I had unknowingly set myself up for. Life is whatever we make it to be. If we go through life with the mindset that life is a series of endless problems to be solved, one after another, then it becomes so for us. Yet if we go through life with the mindset that life is one great experience after another, our outer reality mirrors our inner beliefs. Life becomes whatever we choose it to be.

Since I've consciously adopted this new way of living, I haven't encountered a "problem" in years. They just miraculously melted away from my life. I remember thinking that life was always one set of problems after another and wondering when it would all end. Now I realize that I was the one perpetuating and attracting all those problems all along! The Universe does not perceive any problem that needs to be solved from its perspective, so nothing we do will ever convince the Universe that we have a "problem." In fact, the harder one tries to convince the Universe that they have a problem, the more the problem becomes solidified in one's outer reality, because we expend so much effort justifying the existence of the problem itself!

This is an important spiritual principle to realize. Although I used the words "problem-solving" in the heading of this chapter, I would like to encourage you to shift your perception of what problems really are. This is not merely just a play on words or perspective, but a seldom-understood piece of the spiritual puzzle. Problems represent blind spots in our own thinking. I once heard a wonderful saying: "A problem is merely a question that you have not yet found the answer to." Once you find the solution, it is no longer a problem. In my book "Manifestation Pathways," I explain that infinite pathways always exist between you and your desired good. If that's the case, then there is a solution to all of our problems, somewhere. Knowing that a solution *always* exists, is it still a problem? In fact, I would argue that if you knew with certainty that every single problem in your life would eventually be resolved...then you really have no problems to begin with!

The studying of these spiritual laws will help you reach this realization sooner or later, when you realize that everything is perfect the way it is, and that there really are no "problems" out there to be solved. All of our perceived problems are really within us, and represent sticking points in our own thinking. It is when we think that our problems are unsolvable that we worry over them.

Therefore, the first rule of spiritual problem-solving is really this: A problem represents an undesired situation in your current reality. In order to shift this undesired reality into something more desired, there is no need to reinforce the existence of the problem by describing it in detail or justifying why you should *not* have it. Instead, the art of spiritual problem-solving requires that you place absolutely **no attention** on the problem at all, and instead move directly into a vibrational frequency that is in line with the solution.

Let me first explain this in terms of an everyday example. Suppose that you are learning about a particular subject for the first time and you are curious about what you are learning. It may be geography, history or the sciences. When you are in questioning mode, your mind generates lots of questions, one after another. You are curious to know more about various aspects of what you are learning. Young children are frequently in questioning mode, coming up with one question after another (which often ticks the adults off!). Think back to a time when you were in questioning mode yourself; genuinely curious about the subject you were learning. *Feel* how you felt when you were in questioning mode.

Now think of another time in your life when you were in answering mode. Perhaps you were explaining a subject about which you are quite knowledgeable to a friend, or guiding a co-worker along at the workplace. Or perhaps you were providing justifications for a new project. *Feel* how this answering mode feels to you.

Do you feel the inner differences between being in a questioning and an answering mode? You would have noticed that these two modes felt vastly differently on the inside. When you are asking questions, it is difficult to generate answers. Similarly, when you are generating answers, it is difficult to come up with questions. You may find answers to questions coming easily to you when you are in answering mode. But when you are in questioning mode, a question usually leads to more and more follow-up questions.

The divergent nature of these two inner modes ties in perfectly with our earlier discussion. Most people think they are in answering mode when they think about and focus on their problems. However, once they pay attention to the way they feel on the inside, they will notice that they are really in questioning mode. A focus on the problem brings about more associated negative thoughts about the problem, which moves us further away from our desired solutions.

In my early days, I was often concerned about my financial situation. I was always afraid of running out of money (the perceived problem), therefore I devoted a large amount of my time and mental energy to "solving" this problem. I was determined to overcome it! In fact, I spent almost every single waking hour worrying about my finances, trying to come up with ways to earn more money. My inner state back then was fraught with fears, worries and doomsday scenarios. If you had asked me what I was doing back then, I would have said I was finding a solution to my problems. The truth is that I was doing everything *but* that! By allowing myself to remain continually fixated on the problem, I was actually perpetuating the problem without realizing it.

Is it possible for someone in my shoes to quickly turn around their financial (or any other undesired) situation? Absolutely yes, and it forms the crux of these teachings. If I had allowed myself to dwell entirely on the solutions (desired realities) back then, paying absolutely no attention to the undesired circumstances in my life, my situation would have turned around within a very short time! When I finally applied these principles to my own life, all of the previous problems which had seemed so insurmountable to me straightened themselves out within an astonishingly short time. I had never imagined I would be free from some of the biggest issues in my life in just a few weeks. It can be the same for you, too.

Let's get right down to using these non-verbal protocols for directed problem-solving. Suppose that there is a particular situation in your life right now that is causing you considerable distress, which you would like to change. Remind yourself that how you got here is not important. It is the willingness to change that matters. Therefore, there is no need to analyze the situation in great detail and to find out why it happened. You do not need to know the *whys* in order to shift the undesired situation. This is another key point, because I often see people getting lost in the *whys* of their problem. They are so determined to find out the root causes that they just perpetuate the issue even further. Each time you ask "why" or "why me," you slip into questioning mode that brings you further away from the desired solutions.

This is also the same reason why spiritual healers are often not interested in knowing about the "history" of your health problems or issues. Some of them don't even want to know what symptoms or conditions you have. An effective spiritual healer (manifestor) is one who is able to focus entirely on the desired outcome, to the exclusion of everything else. This is what we are going to do next.

Suppose that you are in the middle of a situation that distresses you. You may be in the middle of an argument with your spouse or co-worker, or suddenly gripped by a deep sense of panic over an issue in your life. This is when your awareness of the problem becomes particularly acute and when you feel the most negative emotions. In times like this when the problem becomes particularly apparent for you, it is not a good idea to try these non-verbal protocols directly. Instead, you would want to cool off and distract yourself for a moment or two until you are calm enough to apply the process.

The moment you feel better and have some personal space to apply the process, sit quietly by yourself and close your eyes. Take a few deep breaths, breathing out slowly each time. Take as many deep breaths as necessary until you feel your body physically relax and your heart rate start to decrease. There is no need to rush through the process, so take as much time as you like to get into a relaxed and comfortable state.

The non-verbal protocol to solve any kind of perceived problem in your life is **solutions space (SS).** The purpose of this non-verbal protocol is not to come up with the solution, but to connect vibrationally with the space in which all solutions (and therefore *your* particular solution) exists.

Once you are in a relaxed and comfortable position, gently feel how it would be to have the "problem" completely resolved. Now this is where practice becomes useful. You'll want to practice this on smaller issues first before moving on to bigger issues. In gently feeling the problem completely resolved, there is no need to know exactly what the solution will be. Therefore, there is a distinction here between non-verbally *feeling* the solution, and *knowing* in detail what the solution is. You can *feel* the solution without knowing what it is, and this is the key.

Most people will say, "But I can't feel the solution without knowing what it is, or at least having a clear view of it!" This is exactly what is keeping your desired solution from coming to you. In my early days, I would say, "But I cannot feel better about my situation unless I have one or two tangible ideas I know would work!" That's not how the Universe works. You must be in vibrational harmony with the frequency of the solution first, before the solution can present itself to you. And this is the biggest secret—you can be in vibrational harmony with the solution *even if* you have absolutely no clue what the solution is going to be! All you need to do is to get in touch with **solutions space (SS)**, the space where all solutions and possibilities exist.

This is key: while you are in that calm and peaceful state, gently allow yourself to feel the solution (whatever it may be) purely in your inner state, without the use of any thoughts or words. Note that you are feeling for the solutions space, the place where your situation is resolved and all the answers exist. You are not feeling to *know* or to *derive* what the specific solution to your problem may be. This is a very important distinction.

Some people may have difficulty doing this the first time round. If so, it is important to take a step back and ask yourself if you're trying too hard to find the right solution. Again, remember that we are not trying to find a solution here. We are trying to find out what the solution *feels like* and then amplify those feelings within our inner state. There is a subtle yet important difference between the two.

The longer you have been stuck with a perceived problem, the more difficult it may be to feel what the solution feels like. Many people stuck with problems in their lives have never felt how the solutions would feel for them, because they are unwilling to even entertain that possibility in their consciousness! But this is the secret—the solutions space, the place where all the answers you are looking for are held, exists somewhere in an alternate reality. It is possible to get in touch with this solutions space vibrationally through your non-verbal feelings *first*, even before you have any inkling of what the situation will be. Conversely, once you get in touch with the solutions space through the power of your intent and feelings, then the solutions have to come flooding very quickly into your life.

I have seen this work one hundred percent of the time in my own life. In times when the solutions were slow to come, it was always a part of myself that was blocking the change. Either I did not believe that change in that area was truly possible, or I did not make the effort to *feel* for the solutions space. Once you resolve these two inner blocks within yourself, the solutions have to come very easily to you.

If you have trouble getting in touch with the solutions space within a single sitting, it is alright. Resume your practice at another time. Each time, try to get in touch with the solutions space a little more. Remember to ignore all thoughts and drop the use of words completely in your consciousness. Instead, just focus on holding the feelings associated with the solutions space. When that feeling comes through very strongly for you on the inside, then a probable solution is not far off for you on the outside.

There was once a time that I was struggling with a tricky work-related problem that had far-reaching consequences for my career, along with an urgent deadline. I stopped myself from applying this technique because I reasoned that this technique will not help me to get the ideas I needed. Notice how I was unconsciously sabotaging my own efforts here? Finally, out of sheer desperation and having tried everything humanly possible, I applied this non-verbal protocol for directed problem-solving just before I went to bed one night. It quickly became apparent why I felt so stuck when I dealt with the problem intellectually. I realized that I could not *feel* for the solutions space at all. Deep within myself, I had a strong unconscious belief that there was no solution to this problem! No wonder logical problem-solving attempts using my conscious mind yielded nothing.

What I did during the session was merely to get in touch with the solutions space, the place where all solutions exist. It took some persistence because I could not *feel* any solutions in the first five to ten minutes I tried this process. But I kept at it. Eventually, I was able to *feel* a bit of the solution within myself and gradually amplify those feelings. Note that I still did not know *what* the solution would actually be, but that's not the key here. When you get in touch with the solutions vibrationally, they have to appear very quickly in your outer reality. Sure enough, the desired answers came through (seemingly out of the blue) the next day, while I was sketching my options on paper. The answers came into my physical reality because I was first in touch with the solutions space vibrationally.

So the non-verbal protocol for solving problems in your life, no matter what they may be, is to get in touch with the **solutions space (SS).**

CHAPTER TEN

NON-VERBAL PROTOCOLS FOR PROSPERITY AND ABUNDANCE

Let's now talk about a subject that is close to the hearts of many people—using these spiritual principles for greater abundance and prosperity in one's life. I have written extensively about this subject in two of my previous books, namely "Banned Money Secrets" and "Dollars Flow to Me Easily," so do read those books if you would like a primer on the subject of spiritual abundance. In this chapter, I would like to focus on an application of the thoughtless manifestations process and how it relates to creating more financial abundance in our lives.

A gentle reminder though, if you skipped right to this chapter without reading the first half of this book, you will have missed out on some of the fundamental skills needed for this process. Be sure to read this book from the beginning. It will be well worth your time and effort. I promise you'll be well-equipped and ready to apply the process when you finally reach this chapter!

Manifesting more abundance and prosperity is no different from manifesting any other tangible object or intangible experience in your life. The Universe does not distinguish between the actual content of your desires. It does not care (or give you a more difficult time) just because you asked for money over a bar of chocolate. However, the reason why manifesting money *seems* more difficult than a bar of chocolate is because of our preconceived expectations and beliefs about the process.

Many people have trouble manifesting more financial abundance because of the overwhelmingly negative emotional baggage surrounding the subject of money. Each of us has our own hang-ups (blind spots) when it comes to money. We may have picked them up through our own personal experiences or absorbed them through societal conditioning. No matter what baggage or negative beliefs we are currently holding about money, they can always be gently released and let go of in favor of more resourceful beliefs.

The reason why there is no one-size-fits-all approach to manifesting money is because we are all at different stages of our journey. Similarly, we all perceive the role of money differently in our lives. I once thought that *everyone* wanted to be rich. Why not? Having lots of money seemed like a dream come true for me back then and I presumed that everyone else would want the same thing.

Studying and applying these spiritual laws opened my mind. I found my own perspective about money shifting over time. Upon examining my own beliefs more closely, I realized that I wanted "lots of money" because I was feeling insecure and fearful about money most of the time. Hence I perceived that having lots of money would be the perfect solution to my worries. But was it really?

Suppose that I somehow managed to come into contact with a large sum of money back then—say, by winning the lottery. Do you think all my money problems would have been solved? They might have been, for a short while. But without really correcting what happens on the inside, I can assure you that my outer reality would revert back to the same picture of worry and lack within a short time. In fact, this was precisely what I experienced. Each manifestation technique I tried brought me *some* success, but I always found myself needing to use it again after the money was spent. In other words, I kept creating lackful experiences in my outer reality, because my inner state was steeped in fears and worries about lack.

When using these non-verbal protocols to create more wealth and financial abundance, one must be mindful of where they currently are along their journey. For example, are you constantly worried about money? Are you always worried about not having enough to pay the bills? If so, it will help if you use the thought-less manifestations process to deal with these constant negative feelings first, *before* using them to ask for money. On the other hand, if your inner state is largely free from fears and worries, then you can use the process to generate more options and possibilities. You will find the thought-less manifestations process useful for you wherever you are on your journey, but you first have to apply it in an appropriate manner for the fastest possible results. You have to use the right intention for your specific circumstances.

Let's suppose that you are worried about money most of the time. One immediate benefit of the thought-less manifestations process is that it can be used to instantly quell your fears and worries about money. Some people may say, "What use does quelling my fears and worries on the inside have? It does not change my outer financial circumstances!" This is a point which I have repeatedly made in all of my previous books, and it is worth repeating here: When you take care of whatever happens on the inside, then your outer reality (which is really a mirror of your inner state) **has to** straighten itself out. In other words, if you focus on tending to your inner state on the inside, then whatever perceived problems and circumstances you have on the outside will soon fade away. The only way this will not work for you is if you refuse to try it for yourself.

Back when I was constantly worried about money, I was always focused on various actions and steps that I could take to make more money. To me, dealing with my worries on the inside was the last thing I would ever do. I often justified my perspective with, "Of course I would be worried about money! That's why I'm taking all these steps to make more of it!" I did not realize back then that had I dealt with the worries *first*, all the problems in my outer reality would subsequently resolve themselves as I later found out. If this is something difficult for you to do at this time, then do both. Deal with your inner worries and at the same time take any physical actions which you feel compelled to. In time, you'll realize that it was your inner steps (and not your outer physical actions) that made the difference.

How does one use these non-verbal protocols to deal with inner fears and worries? It is simple. The non-verbal protocol to use here is **Peace About My Finances (PAMF)**. Forget about asking for more money or for greater abundance to come into your life. The various manifestations will show up once you deal with the negative and worried feelings first, and the best way to do so is to use the **PAMF** protocol. Repeat the protocol three times daily, for about five minutes each time, until you feel differently about your financial situation. It is true that your outer reality will still seem to be the same in the beginning, but you would have shifted on the inside, and that is enough to create an outer change.

If you continue to apply the **PAMF** protocol with consistency over the next few weeks, you will start seeing actual evidence of financial manifestations that will in turn soothe your feelings about your finances more. Applying the **PAMF** protocol was all it took to turn my finances around. That was when people started knocking on my doors and giving me business, without me having to go out and ask for any of it. Once you take this first step on the inside, things become so much easier on the outside.

Suppose that you have dealt with all (or most) of your worries about your finances. This is when your outer reality begins to shift. It is also at this point where you will find most of your intentions and desires taking shape for you in the form of outer manifestations. Because you no longer spend your energy and focus worrying over your undesired outcomes, you will have freed up lots of space in your consciousness which can used for other creative endeavors. Therefore, a spontaneous spike in creativity is common here.

The question of "What's next?" often comes up for individuals who have experienced this transformation. I would encourage you to apply the **Infinite Possibilities (IP)** protocol for generating new possibilities and options in your life as you move forward powerfully. Hold an intention to experience infinite possibilities. You'll be surprised at how much of life remains to be explored and how much is still possible when you show your willingness to joyfully go forward into more exhilarating adventures!

At times, you may feel that the outer changes are happening too quickly and beyond your control. Of course, we always get what we ask for but when good (or supposedly bad) things happen in droves, it can be unnerving for certain individuals. Many spiritual students who apply these techniques often find themselves faced with drastic and huge manifestations, both wanted and unwanted. This is because once you have reached a state of peace about your situation and when there are no longer any inner blocks obstructing your outer manifestations, what you have consciously or unconsciously asked for in the past will come flooding into your experience very quickly.

To regulate this experience, especially if you feel unnerved by the changes, use the **Everything Happens In My Highest Good** or **My Highest Good (MHG)** protocol. This is an especially useful intention to hold when going through times of change. You can also use the following protocol, which I adopted from one of Louise Hay's beautiful affirmations: "I am in the rhythm and flow of ever-changing life." In this case, the non-verbal protocol would be **In The Flow (ITF)**. Hold an intention to always be in the flow of life.

Finally, for longstanding manifestations that have been slow in coming, you can apply the following non-verbal protocols to prevent self-sabotage:

Use the **Open, Allowing And Receptive To All Good (OAR or OAR TAG)** protocol to open yourself up to receiving all good in your life. Simply by holding an intention for **OAR TAG**, you allow the changes and improvements which you have asked for but have unconsciously resisted to come into your life.

For example, I once held an intention for increased business revenue. Yet at the same time, I held myself back from investing in certain new projects because of the initial capital outlay needed, although they could have paid off handsomely if things had worked out. As a result of these two conflicting intentions, I hesitated and did nothing. This is an example of how we can sometimes unconsciously block our good intentions in a certain area of our life by acting in ways that are contrary to our primary intention. Using the **OAR** non-verbal protocol will make you more aware of such instances. When I realized I was unconsciously sabotaging myself through an irrational fear of loss, I was able to let go of my fears and worries associated with losing money and confidently proceed with those investment projects, which in turn opened more doors for me.

Chapter Eleven

Non-Verbal Protocols for Health and Healing

Health is an integral part of life. It is the foundation upon which everything else is built. Indeed, without a fit and healthy physical body, one would find it difficult to enjoy all the material riches that are piled onto us. We experience and enjoy the world around us through our physical bodies. Individuals faced with an illness often wish they could exchange their material wealth for their health, lamenting how they should have taken better care of their bodies. It is often in moments of illness that material riches seem so insignificant. This suggests that most people perceive material riches and health as some sort of a trade-off, in which you can either have wealth or health, but not both. This perspective cannot be further from the great spiritual truth.

It is possible to be in great health and enjoy great wealth at the same time. Millions of people around the world have done it. Many of them are ordinary folks just like you and me. Take a look around and you will find evidence of people who are enjoying great health *and* wealth. Ask the Universe to show such evidence to you and make an intention to learn from these people who have mastered the art of life. One does not have to trade one for the other. You can live the best life and have the best experiences right here in this lifetime.

Few people realize that ailments and illnesses are also physical manifestations, albeit undesired ones. Our physical body bears the brunt of our negative thoughts, beliefs and feelings, because we move around in it all the time. Think of how the outer body of your car shields you from the elements during your daily travels. In return, it becomes damaged by stone chips, rain, hail or snow. Similarly, the interior of your car suffers from wear and tear with frequent use.

In the same way, our body is constantly picking up on every single thought, word, deed and belief that we hold about ourselves and the world around us. It's little wonder that our bodies become battered after a while if we do not nourish them! Much of the damage comes from our negative feelings and thoughts. Our bodies are not impervious to the energetic and vibrational effects of our thoughts, words and deeds. Our bodies are the first to experience the effects of our emotions.

It helps to view the body as an energetic system. This is the basic model which spiritual and energy healers throughout the ages have worked with. Therefore, any positive or negative thought, when held for prolonged periods of time in our consciousness has the ability to affect our body. The consequences of holding onto perpetually negative thoughts include the unwanted manifestation of illnesses and diseases. Louise Hay's "You Can Heal Your Life" is an excellent classic about the connection between our long-held thoughts and physical manifestations of various ailments in our bodies.

It is important to recognize that no matter what physical condition you think you have today, it can always be reversed. It is not permanent. Your body's natural state of being is one of optimal and perfect health. Therefore, any illness that detracts you from enjoying that state of optimal health is only temporary and can always be reversed, by eliminating the causes of that illness. Very often, these causes are emotional in nature and can be corrected simply by going within. Lester Levenson, creator of the Sedona Method, suffered from so many physical ailments that he was sent home from the hospital to await death at the age of 42! Imagine receiving such a devastating death sentence just as you are going through the prime of life. He was outwardly successful, but spiritually empty on the inside. Fortunately for the rest of us, he discovered the Sedona Method for letting go of negative feelings, which not only corrected all of his physical ailments, but also allowed him to perceive the true nature of our Universe.

Even supposedly "incurable" illnesses such as cancer can be reversed. One of the most riveting testimonies I have read is from the book "Dying to Be Me," written by Anita Moorjani. Although Anita was not particularly spiritual while growing up, her near-death experience corresponds with many of the spiritual principles that Louise Hay or Lester Levenson have spoken about.

All of this evidence points to one fundamental truth: your body has the ability to heal itself and correct any perceived ailments, **if you let it**. We sabotage our own healing by allowing ourselves to hold on to negative thoughts and destructive habits. The moment we let all of these negative limiting beliefs go, divine intelligence takes over and keeps everything running in optimal health. This is similar to what spiritual healers do: they serve as conduits through which Universal divine energy can flow to effect the healing needed. The doctor dresses the wound, but God heals it.

The focus of my books has never been on physical healing. Instead, I have applied these techniques more toward the area of physical manifestations. However, one has to realize that there is essentially no difference between spiritual healing and physical manifestations. A healing *is* a physical manifestation, just as real and possible as manifesting a sum of money or a particular item in your life. Furthermore, the Universe does not distinguish between the actual content of your desires, so it does not matter whether you are asking for a new car or perfect health. They are one and the same.

The thought-less manifestations process can be used to effect physical healing for yourself and your loved ones. The broader principles of manifestation apply here. When a physical symptom becomes particularly obvious and acute for an individual, for example when pain is felt in the body, our natural tendency is to focus wholly on the pain itself. Yet the pain represents an undesired reality which we seek to avoid.

Universal laws suggest that anytime we focus on an undesired reality, we perpetuate that reality and make it even more difficult for outer reality to shift. Now it becomes easy to see when one has been with a physical condition for a long time, why it can be difficult to let the natural healing processes occur. Our natural tendencies to focus on whatever or wherever is hurting takes up almost all of our attention, such that it is impossible to even contemplate an alternate reality.

In other cases, it is not the physical symptoms but our worry over a condition that perpetuates it. For example, you may have just read worrying statistics about the condition which heightens your sense of fear. If you let this sense of fear dominate your consciousness, then you will end up focusing on an undesired reality and perpetuating it unknowingly.

There are two solutions when faced with acute physical symptoms that occupy most of your attention. The first solution is to distract yourself from the symptom. Be creative and find whatever way possible to distract yourself from the pain or from noticing those physical symptoms. Funny movies are a great distraction. If you do this just a little bit more each day, you will find it easier to deliberately redirect your focus from the undesired aspects of reality to the more desired aspects. This is also where prescription drugs can sometimes help. Prescription drugs may lower the severity of our symptoms, such that they become less noticeable to us. As our symptoms become less pronounced, we pay less attention to the undesired aspects of our reality (the illness), which then allows the natural healing process to take place.

The second solution is for someone else to effect healing for an individual. An individual may be too infirm to effect their own healing, and this is where someone else can do it for them. I first touched on this possibility in my book, "The Greatest Gift." The non-verbal protocol to effect healing for someone else is **Perfect Health And Healing (PHH).** More specifically, you can also intend **Perfect Health And Healing for** ___, and fill in the blank with the individual's name. It may seem strange at first to work on an intention for someone else, but it is really the same as holding any other intention on the inside.

When you get to the second stage of the thought-less manifestations process, non-verbally intend **Perfect Health And Healing for** John. Some people will find it more effective to also visualize John in the pink of health, smiling and enjoying life to the fullest. Strengthen that intention on the inside until you feel a sense of inner confirmation. That is when you know it is done, and there is nothing else you need to do. It is important to note that you are not the one doing the healing here. The Universe is always the

one who effects the healing. You are merely helping with the flow of healing energy, which may have
been blocked in some way by John. By strengthening and directing the flow of healing energy toward
John, you are helping John reconnect with the natural healing forces that are already available to him.

It is easy to be attached to the outcome when
applying this non-verbal protocol, especially when
the person we are trying to help is a loved one.
However, understand that the more you try to direct
the process of healing, the more you are interfer-
ing with this divine Universal energy that always
knows what is best. State your intention for perfect
health and then leave it up to the Universe to work
its magic.

Another common question is whether we are
violating the free will of another person when we
do this. Do we need to ask for the patient's permission before we can evoke healing? My current
understanding is that no, we do not need to ask for
someone's permission before carrying out the above
process, just as we do not have to ask for someone's
permission before we bless or think good thoughts
about them. Holding an intention for another person's healing does not take away or diminish their
own free will. On the other hand, it can greatly aid
in their recovery—especially if they are too ill to do
any of this inner work by themselves.

The **Perfect Health And Healing (PHH)** protocol can also be used on yourself. For general mainte-
nance of good health, use the **Perfect Health (PH)**

protocol. There is no need to specifically visualize or intend healing for each part of your body (unless you feel inspired to do so).

Here are three additional protocols related to good health, better energy levels and healthy living:

- **Unlimited Energy (UE)** protocol: To allow a full connection to Universal energy, and to feel energized and revitalized throughout the day.
- **Healing Energy (HE)** protocol: To channel and allow the flow of healing energy throughout your body, or toward a loved one.
- **Loving Energy (LE)** protocol: To channel and allow the flow of loving energy throughout your body, especially useful when healing emotional wounds.

CHAPTER TWELVE

WHAT POSSIBILITIES WILL YOU CREATE FROM HERE?

There you have it—a toolbox for creating your *own* magic and miracles with the thought-less manifestations process. The power of this process comes from dropping all the extraneous thoughts and words usually associated with your intentions, such that what remains is a very powerful, singularly-focused intention.

When you practice the thought-less manifestations process, you may be pleasantly surprised by the short amount of time it takes before you observe changes in your outer reality. Because your intentions are no longer contradicted by various counter-intentions and negative thoughts, physical manifestations happen much more effectively and expediently for you. You no longer have to repeatedly ask for what you want. Instead, all you have to do is to hold a pure and light intention for something on the inside, and the corresponding manifestations occur on the outside.

I have been sharing these spiritual principles for the longest time. Before I discovered the thought-less manifestations method, it used to be difficult to concentrate and focus purely on holding a powerful intention on the inside. Now with the thought-less manifestations method and these non-verbal protocols, the whole manifestations process becomes easier than ever before. I am delighted in the new possibilities that are shown to me as I play with this technique in my daily life, and I am excited for the possibilities that will come next for you.

Use what I have written and shared in this book as a starting point. This is not the last word on how to apply the thought-less manifestations process. Instead, it is only the beginning. Feel free to create your own non-verbal protocols and share them with other readers of this book in your reviews. Each time you create and access a new non-verbal protocol, you are opening up alternate dimensions in time and space. Each time you share a protocol with others and encourage others to use them, you are inviting the rest of us to play in this alternate dimension which you have created. You are inviting others to join you there.

As more people use these non-verbal protocols, the vibrational frequencies associated with each protocol become stronger and more easily accessible by others. Hence, the power of these non-verbal protocols is greatly compounded if more people tap into them on a regular basis. When you use the non-verbal protocol to improve your own life, you are not only improving your own circumstances, but helping everyone else along the way. Together, the consciousness of our planet and our beliefs of what is possible will be raised.

You have unlimited possibilities ahead of you right now. What possibilities will you choose as part of your new reality? I look forward to joining you in **Infinite Manifestations Space (IMS)**, the place where all manifestations are possible!

About The Author

Richard Dotts is a modern-day spiritual explorer. An avid student of ancient and modern spiritual practices, Richard shares how to apply these timeless principles in our daily lives. For more than a decade, he has experimented with these techniques himself, studying why they work and separating the science from the superstition. In the process, he has created successful careers as an entrepreneur, business owner, author and teacher.

Leading a spiritual life does not mean walking away from your current life and giving up everything you have. The core of his teachings is that you can lead a spiritual and magical life starting right now, from where you are, in whatever field you are in.

You can make a unique contribution to the world, because you are blessed with the abilities of a true creator. By learning how to shape the energy around you, your life can change in an instant, if you allow it to!

Richard is the author of more than 20 Amazon bestsellers on the science of manifestation and reality creation.

An Introduction to the Manifestations Approach of Richard Dotts

Even after writing more than 20 Amazon bestsellers on the subject of creative manifestations and leading a fulfilling life, Richard Dotts considers himself to be more of an adventurous spiritual explorer than a spiritual teacher or "master", as some of his readers have called him by.

"When you apply these spiritual principles in your own life, you will realize that everyone is a master, with no exceptions. Everyone has the power to design and create his own life on his own terms," says Richard.

"Therefore, there is no need to give up your power by going through an intermediary or any spiritual medium. Each time you buy into the belief that your good can only come through a certain teacher or a certain channel…you give up the precious opportunity to realize your own good. My best teachers were those who helped me recognize the innate power within myself, and kept the faith for me even when I could not see this spiritual truth for myself."

Due to his over-questioning and skeptical nature (unaided by the education which he received over the years), Richard struggled with the application of these spiritual principles in his early years.

After reading thousands of books on related subjects and learning about hundreds of different spiritual traditions with little success, Richard realized there was still one place left unexplored.

It was a place that he was the most afraid to look at: **his inner state.**

Richard realized that while he had been applying these Universal principles and techniques dutifully on the outside, his inner state remained tumultuous the whole time. Despite being well-versed in these spiritual principles, he was constantly plagued with negative feelings of worry, fear, disappointment, blame, resentment and guilt on the inside during his waking hours. These negative feelings and thoughts drained him of much of his energy and well-being.

It occurred to him that unless he was free from these negative feelings and habitual patterns of thought, any outer techniques he tried would not work. That was when he achieved his first spiritual breakthrough and saw improvements in his outer reality.

Taking A Light Touch

The crux of Richard's teachings is that one has to do the inner work first by tending to our own inner states. No one else, not even a powerful spiritual master, can do this for us. Once we have restored our inner state to a place of *zero*, a place of profound calmness and peace…that is when miracles can happen. Any subsequent intention that is held with <u>a light touch</u> in our inner consciousness quickly becomes manifest in our outer reality.

Through his books and teachings, Richard continually emphasizes the importance of taking a light touch. This means adopting a carefree, playful and detached attitude when working with these Universal Laws.

"Whenever we become forceful or desperate in asking for what we want, we invariably delay or withhold our own good. This is because we start to feel even more negative feelings of desperation and worry, which cloud our inner states further and prevent us from receiving what we truly want."

To share these realizations with others, Richard has written a series of books on various aspects of these manifestation principles and Universal Laws. Each of his books touches on a different piece of the manifestation puzzle that he has struggled with in the past.

For example, there are certain books that guide readers through the letting-go of negative feelings and the dropping of negative beliefs. There are books that talk about how to deal with self-doubt and a lack of faith in the application of these spiritual principles. Yet other books offer specific techniques for holding focused intentions in our inner consciousness. A couple of books deal with advanced topics such as nonverbal protocols for the manifestation process.

Richard's main goal is to break down the mysterious and vast subject of spiritual manifestations into easy to understand pieces for the modern reader. While he did not invent these Universal Laws and is certainly not the first to write about them, Richard's insights are valuable in showing readers how to easily apply these spiritual principles despite leading modern and hectic lifestyles. Thus, a busy mother of three or the CEO of a large corporation can just as easily access these timeless spiritual truths through Richard's works, as an ancient ascetic who lived quietly by himself.

It is Richard's intention to show readers that miracles are still possible in our modern world. When you experience the transformational power of these teachings for yourself, you stop seeing them as unexpected miracles and start seeing them as part of your everyday reality.

Do I have to read every book in order to create my own manifestation miracles?

Because Richard is unbounded by any spiritual or religious tradition, his work is continuously evolving based on a fine-tuning of his own personal experiences. He does, however, draw his inspiration from a broad range of teachings. Richard writes for the primary purpose of sharing his own realizations and not for any commercial interest, which is why he has shied away from the publicity that typically comes with being a bestselling author.

All of his books have achieved Amazon bestseller status with no marketing efforts or publicity, a testament to the effectiveness of his methods. An affiliation with a publishing house could mean a pressure to write books on certain popular subjects, or a need to censor the more esoteric and non-traditional aspects of his writing. Therefore, Richard has taken great steps to ensure his freedom as a writer. It is this freedom that keeps him prolific.

One of Richard's aims is to help readers apply these principles in their lives with minimal struggle or strain, which is why he has offered in-depth guidance on many related subjects. Richard himself has maintained that there is no need to read each and every single one of his books. Instead, one should just narrow in to the particular aspects that they are struggling with.

As he explains in his own words, "You can read just one book and completely change your life on the basis of that book if you internalized its teachings. You can do this not only with my books, but also with the books of any other author."

"For me, the journey took a little longer. One book could not do it for me. I struggled to overcome years of negative programming and critical self-talk, so much so that reading thousands of books did not help me as well. But after I reached that critical tipping point, when I finally 'got it', then I started to get everything. The first book, the tenth book, the hundredth book I read all started to make sense. I could pick up any book I read in the past and intuitively understand the spiritual essence of what the author was saying. But till I reached that point of understand within myself, I could not do so."

Therefore, one only needs to read as many books as necessary to achieve a true understanding on the inside. Beyond that, any reading is for one's personal enjoyment and for a fine-tuning of the process.

Which book should I start with?
There is no prescribed reading order. Start with the book that most appeals to you or the one that you feel most inspired to read. Each Richard Dotts book is self-contained and is written such that the reader can instantly benefit from the teachings within, no matter which stage of life they are at. If any prerequisite or background knowledge is needed, Richard will suggest additional resources within the text.

OTHER BOOKS
BY RICHARD DOTTS

Many of these titles are progressively offered in various formats (both in hard copy and eBook). Our intention is to eventually make all these titles available in hard copy format.

- **Banned Manifestation Secrets**
  It all starts here! In this book, Richard lays out the fundamental principles of spiritual manifestations and explains common misconceptions about the "Law of Attraction." This is also the book where Richard first talks about the importance of one's inner state in creating outer manifestations.
- **Come and Sit With Me (Book 1): How to Desire Nothing and Manifest Everything**
  If you had one afternoon with Richard Dotts, what questions would you ask him about manifesting your desires and the creative process? In Come and Sit With Me, Richard candidly answers some of the most pressing questions that have been asked by his readers. Written in a

RichardDottsRichardDottsRichardDotts

RICHARD DOTTS

free-flowing and conversational format, Richard addresses some of the most relevant issues related to manifestations and the application of these spiritual principles in our daily lives. Rather than shying away from tough questions about the manifestation process, Richard dives into them head-on and shows the readers practical ways in which they can use to avoid common manifestation pitfalls.

- **The Magic Feeling Which Creates Instant Manifestations**
  Is there really a "magic feeling", an inner state of mind that results in almost instant manifestations? Can someone live in a perpetual state of grace, and have good things and all your deepest desires come true spontaneously without any "effort" on your part? In this book, Richard talks about why the most effective part of visualizations lies in the *feelings*...and how to get in touch with this magic feeling.

- **Playing In Time And Space: The Miracle of Inspired Manifestations**
  In Playing In Time And Space, Richard Dotts shares the secrets to creating our own physical reality from our current human perspectives. Instead of seeing the physical laws of space and time as restricting us, Richard shares how anyone can transcend these perceived limitations of space and time by changing their thinking, and manifest right from where they are.

108

- **Allowing Divine Intervention**

  Everyone talks about wanting to live a life of magic and miracles, but what does a miracle really look like? Do miracles only happen to certain spiritual people, or at certain points in our lives (for example, at our most desperate)? Is it possible to lead an everyday life filled with magic, miracles and joy?

  In Allowing Divine Intervention, Richard explains how miracles and divine interventions are not reserved for the select few, but can instead be experienced by anyone willing to change their current perceptions of reality.

- **It is Done! The Final Step To Instant Manifestations**

  The first time Richard Dotts learnt about the significance of the word "Amen" frequently used in prayers…goosebumps welled up all over his body and everything clicked in place for him. Suddenly, everything he had learnt up to that point about manifestations made complete sense.

  In It Is Done!, Richard Dotts explores the hidden significance behind these three simple words in the English language. Three words, when strung together and used in the right fashion, holds the keys to amazingly accurate and speedy manifestations.

- **Banned Money Secrets**

  In Banned Money Secrets of the Hidden Rich, Richard explains how there is a group of individuals in our midst, coming from almost every walk of life, who have developed a special relationship with money. These are the individuals for whom money seems to flow easily at will, which has allowed them to live exceedingly creative and fulfilled lives unlimited by money. More surprisingly, Richard discovered that there is not a single common characteristic that unites the "hidden rich" except for their unique ability to focus intently on their desires to the exclusion of everything else. Some of the "hidden rich" are the most successful multi-millionaires and billionaires of our time, making immense contributions in almost every field.

Richard teaches using his own life examples that the only true, lasting source of abundance comes from behaving like one of the hidden rich, and from developing an extremely conducive inner state that allows financial abundance to easily flow into your life.

- **The 95-5 Code: for Activating the Law of Attraction**
Most books and courses on the Law of Attraction teach various outer-directed techniques one can use to manifest their desires. All is well and good, but an important question remains unanswered: What do you do during the remainder of your time when you are not actively using these manifestation techniques? How do you live? What do you do with the 95% of your day, the majority of your waking hours when you are not actively asking for what you want? Is the "rest of your day" important to the manifestation process?

It turns out that what you do during the 95% of your time, the time NOT spent visualizing or affirming, makes all of the difference.

In The 95-5 Code for activating the Law of Attraction, Richard Dotts explains why the way you act (and feel) during the majority of your waking hours makes all the difference to your manifestation end results.

- **Inner Confirmation for Outer Manifestations**

How do you know if things are on their way after you have asked for them?

What should you do after using a particular manifestation technique?

What does evidence of your impending manifestations feel like?

You may not have seen yourself as a particularly spiritual or intuitive person, much less an energy reader…but join Richard Dotts as he explains in Inner Confirmation for Outer Manifestations how everyone can easily perceive the energy fields around them.

- **Mastering the Manifestation Paradox**

The Manifestation Paradox is an inner riddle that quickly becomes apparent to anyone who has been exposed to modern day Law of Attraction and manifestation teachings. It is an inner state that seems to be contradictory to the person practicing it, yet one that is associated with inevitably fast physical manifestations—that of *wanting* something and yet at the same time *not wanting* it.

Richard Dotts explains why the speed and timing of our manifestations depends largely on our mastery of the Manifestation Paradox. Through achieving a deeper understanding of this paradox, we can consciously and deliberately move all our desires (even those we have been struggling with) to a "sweet spot" where physical manifestations *have to occur* very quickly for us instead of having our manifestations happen "by default."

- **Today I Am Free: Manifesting Through Deep Inner Changes**

  In Today I Am Free, Richard Dotts returns with yet another illuminating discussion of these timeless Universal Laws and spiritual manifestation principles. While his previous works focused on letting go of the worry and fear feelings that prevent our manifestations from happening in our lives, Today I Am Free focuses on a seldom discussed aspect of our lives that can affect our manifestations in a big way: namely our interaction with others and the judgments, opinions and perceptions that other people may hold of us. Richard Dotts shows readers simple ways in which they can overcome their constant feelings of fear and self-consciousness to be truly free.

- **Dollars Flow To Me Easily**

  Is it possible to read and relax your way into financial abundance? Can dollars flow to you even if you just sat quietly in your favorite armchair and did "nothing"? Is abundance and prosperity really our natural birthright, as claimed by so many spiritual masters and authors throughout the ages?

Dollars Flow To Me Easily takes an alternative approach to answering these questions. Instead of guiding the reader through a series of exercises to "feel as if" they are already rich, Richard draws on the power of words and our highest intentions to dissolve negative feelings and misconceptions that block us from manifesting greater financial abundance in our lives.

- **Light Touch Manifestations: How To Shape The Energy Field To Attract What You Want**
Richard covers the entire manifestation sequence in detail, showing exactly how our beliefs and innermost thoughts can lead to concrete, outer manifestations. As part of his approach of taking a light touch, Richard shows readers how to handle each component of the manifestation sequence and tweak it to produce fast, effective manifestations in our daily lives.

- **Infinite Manifestations: The Power of Stopping at Nothing**
In Infinite Manifestations, Richard shares a practical, step-by-step method for erasing the unconscious memories and blocks that hold our manifestations back. The Infinite Release technique, "revealed" to Richard by the Universe, is a quick and easy way to let go of any unconscious memories, blocks and resistances that may prevent our highest good from coming to us. When we invoke the Infinite Release process,

we are no longer doing it alone. Instead, we step out of the way, letting go and letting God. We let Universal Intelligence decide how our inner resistances and blocks should be dissolved. All we need to do is to intend that we are clear from these blocks that hold us back. Once the Infinite Release process is invoked, it is done!

- **Let The Universe Lead You!**
  Imagine what your life would be like if you could simply hold an intention for something...and then be led clearly and precisely, every single time, to the fulfilment of your deepest desires. No more wondering about whether you are on the "right" path or making the "right" moves. No more second-guessing yourself or acting out of desperation—You simply set an intention and allow the Universe to lead you to it effortlessly!

- **Manifestation Pathways: Letting Your Good Be There...When You Get There!**
  Imagine having a desire for something and then immediately intuiting (knowing) what the path of least resistance should be for that desire. When you allow the Universe to lead you in this manner and unfold the manifestation pathway of least resistance to you, then life becomes as effortless as knowing what you want, planting it in your future reality and letting your good be there when you get there...every single time! This book shows you the practical techniques to make it happen in your life.

- **And more...**

CPSIA information can be obtained
at www.ICGtesting.com
Printed in the USA
BVHW080209021019
559995BV00015B/204/P

9 781519 125439